□ □ □ □ □ □   **Wisdom to Know**   □

Wisdom to Know

More Daily Meditations for Men

from the Best-Selling Author
of *Touchstones*

Living Solutions
P.O. Box 616, Cork, Ireland.
Tel: INT'L Code + 353 21 4314300
Fax: INT'L Code + 353 21 4961269
e-mail: livhaz@indigo.ie
Website: www.livingsolutions.ie

HAZELDEN ®□

Hazelden
Center City, Minnesota 55012-0176

1-800-328-0094
1-651-213-4590 (Fax)
www.hazelden.org

Library of Congress Cataloging-in-Publication Data

   Wisdom to know : more daily meditations for men /
from the best-selling author of Touchstones.
      p.   cm. — (Hazelden meditations)
   Includes index.
   ISBN-13: 978-1-59285-316-8
   ISBN-10: 1-59285-316-1 (pbk.)
   1. Twelve-step programs—Religious aspects—
Meditations.   2. Prayer-books and devotion—
English.   3. Devotional calendars.   I. Hazelden
Foundation.   II. Series.
   BL624.5.W57 2005
   204'.32—dc22

                                    2005040364

09 08 07 06 05   6 5 4 3 2 1

Cover design by David Spohn
Cover art: *Horizons* by Joseph Jeffers Dodge
Interior design by Ann Sudmeier
Typesetting by Stanton Publication Services, Inc.

Serenity Prayer

God, grant me the serenity
To accept the things I cannot change,
The courage to change the things I can,
And the wisdom to know the difference.

*All the art of living lies in a fine mingling of letting go
and holding on.*

—Havelock Ellis

The wisdom that we attempt to develop in recovery is
how to balance the letting go and the holding on in
our lives. Many of us have sunk into deep holes of crisis and despair by holding on too tightly when we
needed to let go. In other ways, perhaps, we have given
up too easily when, with faith and trust, we could have
held on to opportunities and values that seemed out
of reach.

The Serenity Prayer speaks of the wisdom to know
the difference. This power to discern between what we
must accept and what we can change creates a deep
sense of peace. It brings calm to our intimate partnership, success to our recovery from addiction and codependency, and greater effectiveness in our work life.

*Today I pray for the wisdom to know the difference
between what I must accept and what I can change.*

*Just by speaking I can break out of my self-made
prison.*

—June Singer

For many of us guys, words don't come easily. Maybe
we have strong feelings, strong thoughts, and important things on our mind, but they may not translate
easily into spoken words. Even as toddlers, little boys
don't generally start to speak as early as little girls do.
But that is no excuse for not working at it. Some of
the most difficult challenges produce the most creative
responses.

Something magical happens when the unspoken is
finally spoken. A little of our private world is finally
known by another human being. Even more than that,
we finally know more clearly what is on our minds
when we put words to it and hear ourselves say it. We
may not even know that we are in a self-made prison
of silence until we start to break out of it. Talking—
finding words to say what is on our mind—is a big part
of our healing process.

*Today I will talk to someone about a feeling, a
memory, or an unanswered question.*

Work for something because it is good, not just because it stands a chance of success.

—Vaclav Havel

We are not following the way of the mainstream. Our troubles required us to follow a path of healing and recovery that most of our community and society may not need to follow. A strong message in the world today says that success, in and of itself, is wonderful. On our path, we are always concerned about who we are, not just what we do. We always ask, what is the moral good in our choices? We don't only ask, will it work? Financial success at the expense of our sobriety, serenity, or self-respect is won at far too high a price.

On this path, we ask ourselves daily how we are doing on the moral scale for our lives. Do our choices and our work help create something that is good? Are we following our values or are we just trying to get ahead? Do we treat everyone the way we want to be treated? Are we kind and respectful to the weak as well as the strong? Do we speak the truth when it is called for?

Today I will work for that which is good and leave success in the hands of my Higher Power.

What is laid down, ordered, factual is never enough to embrace the whole truth; life always spills over the rim of the cup.

—Boris Pasternak

We like control. We want to know what to expect. We like to think we have things figured out and know the answers. But God cannot be contained by a human definition—and life will not stay in place after we try to put it there.

When we go to work, we expect our routine to fit the normal pattern, but sometimes surprises await us. When we talk to our partner about an important topic, we expect a certain outcome—but our partner is a separate person with a separate outlook. Something happens that throws us a curve ball. When we accept that life will spill over the rim, there is no need to add our anxiety to the situation. We already know that we cannot contain it, and we learn to go with the flow. We are not in charge of everything, and we never will be. We are not responsible to keep the world on track, only to deal as best we can with what comes our way.

Today, as life spills over the rim of the cup, I will strive to go with the flow.

Many times, when faced with an important decision and no clear idea of the best choice, I have thought, *Please, give me some handwriting on the wall! Make it obvious for me!* But the handwriting never appears, and I have to rely on a less literal, less concrete basis for my choice. Most of life's choices are complex. The alternatives are rarely black and white; the solutions are rarely obvious. We have to turn to something we call wisdom.

The Serenity Prayer is like a thin slice of pie: it's small and simple, but it cuts right to the center. In just a few words, it addresses deep issues of adult life and our need for wisdom to discern our best path. We repeat the Serenity Prayer over and over because it reminds us to make grown-up choices when we face hard situations.

Over the year of writing the meditations in this book, I found myself repeating several themes. One is that masculinity is more about being grown up than it is about being tough and aggressive. Being tough and aggressive are fine traits, but they become brittle and hollow without wisdom, honesty, and respect for self and others.

Another theme that emerged is the image of the healing journey. We are walking a path, and our task is to stay on the path, make progress, have an adventure, and learn the lessons contained in our experiences. We may get off the track at times, find ourselves on a dead end, or get stuck somewhere. Our motto is: Keep coming back. While we walk this path, our goal is not to achieve perfection; it's not even to climb a ladder that leads ever closer to perfection, but simply to keep coming back to the path.

Another theme is awakening our spirituality—experiencing an aliveness and awe for the life we find within and around us. In awakening we find new ways to deal with fear and anger, and we develop wisdom. We don't make ourselves wise by becoming king or master of an unpredictable world. Wisdom comes to us. We become ready for wisdom as we prepare the stage, live by our values, develop self-esteem, and share our lives with others—in relationships and in participation with our group, our family, our community, and our Higher Power. With this wisdom, we experience the truth that we are never alone, and we are better able to navigate through choices where no black or white exists.

Many of my friends and family members have taken an interest in the creation of this book of meditations. They helped by mining their own treasuries of wisdom quotations. Some of them sent me favorite quotes that they kept on their bathroom mirrors or under refrigerator magnets. Others brought their best-loved quotes from personal collections gathered over the years. To all of these friends and loved ones, I say thank you.

M.A.F.

□ □ □ □ □ □   **Wisdom to Know**   □

January

Hope smiles on the threshold of the year to come,
whispering that it will be happier.

—Alfred, Lord Tennyson

At the start of this new year, we look back at what has been and we look forward to the future. Our path has been filled with healing and hope. Rewards have come to us each day. Now, looking toward the year ahead, we can't know much of what will happen, but we can recommit ourselves to our healing and sober path. We can have renewed comfort and optimism that we will not be alone and that we will be able to handle whatever comes our way.

The start of a new year is a good time to make lists of the things we fear, the things we hope for, and the things we are grateful for. These lists serve as a kind of snapshot inventory of our attitude toward the world and our relationship with our Higher Power. They point a direction for us today and for the year ahead. We can put these lists in a safe place until next year when we will bring them out as a reminder of where we were and a measure of how far we've come.

Today I once again turn my life and will over to the care of God.

Nothing is predestined: the obstacles of your past can become gateways that lead to new beginnings.

—Ralph Blum

At this doorway to a new year, we look ahead to new beginnings. In some ways, this is like any other day in the cycle of our lives. Some things we know for sure, and other things are yet to be revealed. We can know that again on this day we will stay sober and true to our path of healing and recovery. Still, we look to the year ahead with a sense of adventure. This year will be a continuing flow of experiences, and on this path we deal with each experience with the calm certainty that we are not alone. We know that we cannot control what happens to us, but we can stay true to ourselves.

"Keep coming back" is a well-known motto for our life in recovery. We are not perfect, and we don't expect perfection of ourselves. What we expect is to keep returning to our path. Like any driver or any pilot who continuously reorients his craft as he travels along his route, we look forward to this year, knowing that we will keep returning to the true course we have chosen. It will be an adventure and we will take whatever happens and use it for our growth.

Living one day at a time, my pledge is to keep coming back to this path of renewal.

*A marriage without conflicts is almost as inconceivable
as a nation without crises.*

—André Maurois

Conflict is not bad; it is necessary. In any good, intimate partnership, the two people reveal themselves to each other. As they reveal themselves, their differences sometimes are interesting and enjoyable and sometimes create conflict. A good conflict is open and honest and without ego. When one person reveals his or her thoughts, the other person listens and hears them as a genuine expression that must be taken into account. The simple act of listening is usually most important; agreement isn't always necessary. Most of the time, a person just wants to be heard. Agreement is required when there is only one path that can be chosen. Then, the wisdom of two loving and honest people can lead to a mutual agreement that often turns out to be better than either individual path.

The true, unique nature of any intimate partnership only takes shape through genuine conflict and resolution. Crises faced and resolved become the foundation for continuing and deepening mutual understanding and intimacy.

*Today I will not avoid conflict but will face it with
honesty and an open heart.*

Be patient with everyone, but above all with yourself.
—Saint Francis de Sales

The path of healing and recovery sets challenging standards. We are asked to "turn our will and our lives over," to be "searching and fearless" in our moral inventory, and to make amends to all those we have harmed. Many of us have lifelong habits of over-criticizing ourselves and condemning ourselves for who we are. When we face challenging standards, we can't meet them perfectly. This is a program of progress, not perfection.

If we are not seeking to attain perfection, then, we need to deepen our understanding of what we *are* seeking. The answer is in the slogan "Keep coming back." It's a slogan usually applied to the idea of continuing to return to meetings, even if we don't see our way clearly at first. But it also applies to meeting standards. We don't seek perfection; we seek to keep coming back to the Steps of recovery because it is a given that we will keep falling off them. It is only when we stop returning to the Steps that we get seriously off track.

Today I will be patient with my progress on this healing journey.

No winter lasts forever; no spring skips its turn.

—Hal Borland

In the midst of winter, the short days and the long nights may seem to last forever. But we know that the turn of the cycle is inevitable. Every winter is followed by spring. When we feel depressed and discouraged, we may not feel optimistic about anything. We may not see the path from here to a place where life feels brighter and warmer. That is when we must remind ourselves that all things eventually change. We do find life beyond our current problems. We do regain our energy and our joy in life.

All pain is finite. It has its beginning and its end. Our path may require us to learn to endure and live with some pain. Some Native Americans' training for youth included fasting and solitary journeys that strengthened them and showed them how to deal with shortage and difficulty. Life must contain dark times, and when we learn that we can carry on until we find light, we have something permanent to fall back on. While we may feel pessimistic, we can remind ourselves that it is only a feature of our current mood, not a permanent state.

Today I live in the knowledge that spring is eternal.

Music washes away from the soul the dust of every-day life.

—Berthold Auerbach

We need ways to express what we have experienced. Expression gives form to our experience and allows us to move on. Music taps into our deeper self and evokes feelings that we may not otherwise have access to. It conveys what is otherwise inexpressible and opens a channel to the spiritual world. Some men love to make music, and all of us can listen to it.

When asked to describe how we make contact with our Higher Power, some men have said that it's mainly through music. The great religious traditions of the world all use music: hymns, bells, chanting, drums. But we don't necessarily need religious music to make conscious contact with our Higher Power. A good song on the radio can do it.

Today I will let music speak for me of things I cannot say in plain words.

If you want others to be happy, practice compassion. If you want to be happy, practice compassion.

—Dalai Lama

The word *compassion* means literally *to suffer with* someone. We normally use the word more broadly to mean empathize, or feel, with a person. Moving out of the prison of our own self-centeredness, we grow in the ability to see the world through the eyes of others. We grow wiser and more effective in our own lives because we aren't limited to one outlook. We learn to forgive ourselves and suddenly we are much freer with our forgiveness of others.

There is a generosity of spirit in compassion, and the most generous attitude comes when we can act compassionately with someone we don't especially like. Even though we may not choose a particular guy to be our best friend, we can accept and honor the hard times he has had and we can put ourselves in his place to see what his challenges have been. Nothing is more admirable than a strong man acting generously and compassionately toward another human being.

Today I will strive to be generous with compassion and to see the world as someone else sees it.

Lead us from the unreal to the real world.

—Hindu invocation

In pursuit of pleasures and escapes during our active addiction, we created a bubble of unreality around ourselves. Stepping into the bubble was exciting; it carried us off into gambling, or erotic and romantic pursuits, or shopping, or drugs and alcohol, or the codependent thrill of scooping other people out of their troubles. We used a whole system of half-truths and self-deceit to allow the bubble to exist. It led us to become more self-centered and more grandiose as we tried to force the unreal world to exist in reality.

Now, as we live in freedom from our addictive and codependent behaviors, we continue to peel back the layers of unreality. We no longer fight with reality as it is, or try to shape and mold it to fit our desires. We see more clearly by living more honestly. One of the benefits of our new life is that we feel clearheaded. Life seems simpler now, and we feel a peace of mind that we could not have even imagined in the past.

May I continue to see and accept reality as it is given.

God's admiration for us is infinitely greater than anything we can conjure up for Him.

—Saint Francis of Assisi

Those of us who look back upon a trail of guilty feelings and shame may find it hard to fathom God's admiration for us. This whole idea, which comes from a Christian saint who lived eight hundred years ago, turns upside down our ideas of a God who is watching us and counting all the things we have done wrong. But we have been created to have a place here. And we have a right to take our place among all of God's beloved creatures.

No matter how imperfect we are, no matter what we feel guilty about, no matter how low our self-esteem, we are living in the grace of a God who loves us and holds us close, even at our lowest point. We sometimes feel alienated from God. We have difficulty making conscious contact. Even then, we can still know that God carries us through these hard times.

Today I will walk in the light of God's admiration and accept it to the best of my ability.

The fearless are merely fearless. People who act in spite of their fear are truly brave.

—James A. LaFond-Lewis

Fear plays a role in our lives in different ways. Many of us have been so conditioned to deny fear that we don't even know we are afraid and are, in fact, reacting to it. We may look back on a major life choice and realize we chose one job over another because of fear. Some of us can see in the rearview mirror that our controlling ways rise out of fear, not desire for power. The fact is that until we allow ourselves to know our fears, we will react impulsively to them and cannot respond bravely to them.

Our fears don't give us a license to control those around us. Our fears don't make our addictive escapes any less harmful. On this path we seek to know our fears, to call them by name so we can be smart in dealing with them. Sometimes we may use our fear as wise guidance to avoid danger, and other times we may choose to bravely step into the circle of our fear and face it down because we do not want to be irrationally ruled by it.

Today I will open my eyes to see my fears and then choose wiser, braver responses to them.

When I hear somebody sigh, "Life is hard," I am always tempted to ask, "Compared to what?"

—Sydney Harris

There is no question—life is hard at times. None of us escapes trials and challenges. And some of us truly seem to have more of them than others. So what are we to do with that realization? We cannot control most of what happens to us. We can only control how we respond to it. No two paths are the same. Self-pity is the response of someone who hasn't yet learned to deal with adult life. Feeling sorry for ourselves is like having a hole in a bucket that allows our spirit and our strength to drain away.

Instead of reacting with self-pity, we remind ourselves that all things change and the difficulty we face today will also change. What is harder for us today will be easier tomorrow. We will have times of peace and satisfaction. Best of all, when we play a bad hand well, we have peace of mind, our inner strength grows, and we have something more in our bank of knowledge.

Today I am grateful for life itself.

Any one thing is "hitched to everything in the universe."

—John Muir

Some days our lives seem to be in chaos. We may feel flooded with too much: too much work, too much pain, too much to learn, or too many problems to handle. On days like this, we can begin to see past the chaos and feel hopeful about dealing with the future because we can turn to our Higher Power.

All things are part of a larger whole in the universe, and all things are connected. We are never completely alone. There is comfort and security in knowing that we can rely on our Higher Power. We only have to do a small part today. The universe will continue to work its way toward a natural solution to today's problems.

Today I will concentrate on simply doing one small part of what needs to be done.

Go confidently in the direction of your dreams! Live the life you've imagined.

—Henry David Thoreau

To have a dream takes courage and a bit of hope. A dream guides us, even if we haven't let ourselves bring it to consciousness. How often do we stop to ask what our dreams are? Do we even know what we want? This path is about becoming the best men we can be. It's more about who we become than what we achieve. So it inspires us to create dreams for our development as men.

When we take a few moments to reflect on the kind of men we want to be, we create reference points, or beacons, to move toward. This gives us a way to measure our actions and our choices. Do our actions take us in the direction we want to go, or do they take us off course? Are we growing into the men we want to be, or have we forgotten to follow our beacons?

In my actions today, I will keep my dreams in mind and choose my course with confidence.

The best inheritance a parent can give his children is a few minutes of his time each day.

—O. A. Battista

As fathers, we have a strong drive to provide for our loved ones. Many of us had fathers who were absent from our daily lives, often because they were working so much. Now, we also may find ourselves so dedicated to making a living and getting ahead that we don't spend much time with our children and all those whom we love. We try to make up for it by giving generous gifts or providing them with many comforts that we didn't have ourselves.

When we get so taken up with our work, we may justify it by saying we are doing it for our families. The truth is, nothing is as valuable as the time we spend together. Children are certainly richer and happier with the nurturing presence of their father than with extra material comforts. We always need to seek a balance. Doing well in our careers has its place, but it isn't the most important thing in life.

I will keep my urge to provide for my loved ones in balance with simply spending time with them.

We must accept finite disappointment, but we must never lose infinite hope.

—Dr. Martin Luther King, Jr.

Hope and freedom and the right to dignity as a man are very personal things for every one of us in recovery. Regardless of our race or creed or ethnic origin, we are alike in that we are walking this healing path out of subjugation to addiction and codependency. Today is the birthday of a heroic man, Dr. Martin Luther King, Jr., who dedicated his life not to his own self-interest, but to peace and the right of all people to be free. He spoke to all people who have struggled under a yoke of pain and trouble.

We must accept disappointments along our path. They are inevitable. We strive hard to achieve a goal and it may slip from our fingers. We fall in love and lose the one we love. In the midst of disappointment we may doubt whether we can handle it. But life goes on. We take our setbacks and ask, *what do I need to learn from this?* We don't lose sight of our long-term objective to become the best kind of man we can be and to live in line with our spiritual principles. That is the path to our personal freedom and dignity.

Today I am grateful that those who have gone before us have shown us the path.

Failure is an event, never a person.

—William D. Brown

At times we have wondered if there is hope for us. But, in fact, we can all succeed in finding peace of mind. We can all achieve self-respect. The most financially successful man may be proud of his achievement but it doesn't satisfy him. By the same token, a major failure doesn't define a man. When we understand that our actions aren't who we are, we will not feel trapped by a failure and we can pursue the greater prize of becoming a better man.

Today we may be troubled by a recent failure or haunted by an old one. We are embarrassed about it and feel we have lost the high regard of our friends. This failure can propel us into greater wisdom and stronger understanding of how to live a life with value.

Today I will take the spiritual leap away from basing my self-esteem on what I do toward basing it on who I am.

*Don't believe that winning is really everything. It's
more important to stand for something. If you don't
stand for something, what do you win?*

—Lane Kirkland

We love competition. Many of us enjoy it both in our
recreation and in our work life. We love to run faster,
play harder, stack higher, pound more, sell more, and
produce more than our friends and business col-
leagues. Some of us seem almost to worship competition as a great virtue, above other virtues such as
camaraderie, teamwork, fair play, community service,
honesty, and generosity. Any good thing can become a
bad thing when it's taken to the extreme. Intemperate
competition serves our primitive, greedy drive for
power. Winning is wonderful—but it is not the only
thing we stand for.

More important than coming out ahead is coming
out with our integrity and self-respect. We preserve our
integrity by adhering to the truth as we know it, caring
for the welfare of others, and dealing fairly and honestly both at work and at play. No win, no personal advantage is ever worth the price of our character.

*Today I will enjoy my competitive side while I uphold
all the other things I stand for.*

The way we see the problem is the problem.

—Stephen R. Covey

Many of us have a mind-set that keeps us on a treadmill. It's not for lack of effort that our lives reel out of control. We struggle to move forward. We work hard to manage the unmanageable. But with all our busy efforts, we can't see that we are continuously recycling the same problem over and over.

The solution we need may be right before our eyes. Our denial is confusing us; we don't even know we are denying anything. We cannot solve our problems alone—or even see the problems clearly from the inside. That's what friends do for us. They reflect back to us what we are missing. That's why we need to have good talks with others who have walked the same path that we are on. The strongest, most powerful men have wise advisers who show them things they don't know. They accept the role of seeker and learner because that is the way they enhance themselves.

Today I will be open to seeing my problems in ways I couldn't imagine on my own.

*For the person who has learned to let go and let be,
nothing can ever get in the way again.*

—Meister Eckhart

We have to learn how to let go. It doesn't come naturally until we have learned how. Letting go is a skill that comes when we see others doing it, and when we practice it. It comes when we accept that we are not completely separate individuals but part of a larger whole. Then we can turn our most vexing problems over to our Higher Power or let others deal with issues that don't belong to us. Most of us worked hard to gain control of our lives and to manage the circumstances we faced. Becoming selective about what we try to control is a very adult skill that takes time and much life experience.

When we can finally let go and stand aside from the things we don't need to manage, we get the payoff of liberation and peace of mind. Our burden is lightened and only the things that we can handle are left.

Today I will take every opportunity to practice the skill of letting go and letting be.

Half this game is ninety percent mental.

—Yogi Berra

A very large part of any addiction is made up of all the thinking and behavior patterns that go with it. Many addictions don't involve alcohol or chemicals at all, just the thoughts and feelings of certain behaviors. Codependency is all about unhealthy thinking. Removing addictive substances is just the start of a long process of changing ourselves mentally.

This mental transformation is the real recovery. It begins as soon as we enter this program, and we feel the rewards very quickly. We are set on a lifelong process of growth that is "ninety percent mental": learning to know our feelings and express them well, relating to other people, trusting others and a Higher Power, and developing healthy attitudes.

Today I will be aware of my mental recovery and notice how much I have already gained.

Where there is great love, there are always wishes.

—Willa Cather

We can always think of ways to improve our intimate partnership, but usually our best ideas are for changes in our partner. We wish we had a more generous attitude from our partner; we wish we had a more agreeable partner—someone who was more fun or who would lose weight—and we want more sexual pleasure. But these ideas are the easy ones to think of. The harder and more effective ideas are those that call for changes in ourselves.

We enter into a life partnership to enjoy the relationship. We take pleasure in each other's lives and we are on the same team. But we don't walk in the same footsteps because we all need to stand on our own as adults. Intimacy is not the merging of personalities but the bridge between separate people. Once we have our adult separateness, we can be more intimate, more loving, and more generous with each other.

Today I will pay more attention to the ways I can be a better partner.

*In the face of uncertainty, there is nothing wrong
with hope.*

—Bernie Siegel

Are we willing to hope? Some of us have adopted an
attitude of optimism about the progress of life. We
know that many things are unpredictable, but we believe we have the strength to deal with whatever happens. Others of us have chosen the opposite. We dare
not hope, protecting ourselves from the hurt of
disappointment. But our spiritual growth calls every
one of us to believe in the possibilities for recovery
and all the promises that go with it.

We need to ask ourselves, *do I dare to hope?* That is
what the Second Step challenges us to do. We simply
suspend our doubts. We put them on the shelf and
hold open the possibility that good things will happen. And if we don't get what we hoped for, we can deal
with it. It is a choice we make.

*Today I will accept the challenge to suspend my doubts
and accept that my life can get better.*

*That old law about "an eye for an eye" leaves
everybody blind.*

—Dr. Martin Luther King, Jr.

Resentment and the urge for revenge can corrode our
lives. We carry these dark feelings with us, sometimes
in the back of our minds and sometimes up front.
Such feelings keep us living in the past and tie us to
the people we resent. Our spiritual goal is to reach the
point of forgiveness. It is not easy to make that transi-
tion, and it cannot be done in a phony way. A good
beginning is first to accept forgiveness as a goal and
then focus our efforts on a thorough and searching inventory of ourselves. Finally, we can reach the point
where we simply tear up the I.O.U. We stop expecting
repayment for past wrongs and release ourselves from
carrying old resentments. We let others deal with their
own God and their own conscience.

We reach a sense of freedom and well-being that is a
great reward for forgiveness. It surprises us when our
own self-esteem rises as we write off the bad debts we
think others owe us.

*Today I am spending my efforts on my own inventory
because that releases me from the burden of the past.*

Journal writing is a voyage to the interior.

—Christina Baldwin

Many men use daily notes in a private journal as a method of meditation. It is a means to learn about themselves as they reflect with pen in hand and put uncensored thoughts down on paper. It can take many forms. Some days a person might just make a list. It might be a prayer list: all the people he loves and all the people he is concerned about. It might be a list of the day's tasks, with notations on the spirit with which to approach them. Some guys draw pictures in their journals and say it helps them quiet their minds and deepen their understanding of a situation. Some simply record the events of the day and then reflect on how they feel about them and what they mean.

Every man in spiritual development needs a daily pattern of meditation and reflection. It should be a gentle means to respect himself, be honest with himself, and hold himself responsible for his life.

Today I will make notes on paper and use my notes to interact with my thoughts.

Wisdom too often never comes, and so one ought not to reject it merely because it comes late.

—Felix Frankfurter

A sure sign of true growth and change is the appearance of regret and grief that such wisdom came so late. Often, when we deeply understand something for the first time or make a real change that improves our lives, we wish we had learned this a long time ago. We mourn the losses and the pain that could have been avoided if we had only seen the light sooner.

However, a good life always brings change and growth. The greatest tragedy is when a man never grows and never sees the light. We always see more clearly after we learn something new, and the regret that accompanies it is inevitable. With enough distance and perspective, most of us reach the point where we say, *I wouldn't change it if I could.*

Today I am grateful for the wisdom I have gained, and I will continue to seek more growth.

You alone can do it, but you cannot do it alone.

—O. Hobart Mowrer

A guy likes to feel independent and self-sufficient. We all naturally want to feel competent and on top of our game. As we live our lives, we gain some savvy about this drive to be our own master. The young boy has a simple idea: the less he needs others, the stronger and better he will be. But the wiser, experienced man knows that a man is stronger and wiser if he is willing to accept the help that is available.

We alone can turn toward the help. We alone can decide to accept what we cannot change. We alone can open ourselves to spiritual grace and stop getting in the way of our Higher Power. The smarter man accepts the paradox that when we take our self-sufficiency too far, we become weaker. We are in the driver's seat when we decide to receive the help of others and our Higher Power.

Today I will open myself to the help that surrounds me.

*When we see men overdoing their masculinity, we can
assume that they . . . are scared that they aren't manly
enough.*

—Frank Pittman

Masculinity is a wonderful thing. It is part of a man's
inner feeling of self-esteem, and it has a wide scope. It's
the feeling that we can protect and provide for ourselves, our family, and our loved ones; that we are
tough when we need to be tough, standing up to difficult challenges; that we are true to our word, loving,
and honorable.

As young boys we had boyish ideas about masculinity. Normally, children have uncomplicated ideas
about life. But boys don't know manhood until they
are there. And some of us didn't have adult men that
we were close to; we couldn't know intimately what
grown men were like. So we reached manhood almost
as outsiders, still trying to fulfill our boyish ideas. We
worked extra hard to fulfill the simple stereotypes of
manhood. That's why we sometimes exaggerated our
behavior like perpetual adolescents, always anxious
about whether our masculinity was measuring up.

We don't need to be anxious about our masculinity.
When we are comfortable that we are man enough, that
we have arrived, there is no need to prove anything.

*Today I value my masculinity and accept myself as a
good man, just as I am.*

*The grand essentials of happiness are: something to do,
something to love, and something to hope for.*

—Allen K. Chambers

A wise old man who had survived years of abuse and
hard labor in a Nazi concentration camp and lost several loved ones to the gas chambers was asked how he
could live without getting depressed. He answered that
it was because he had a purpose in his life.

We are rebuilding our lives after the devastation of
codependency and addiction. The promises of this recovery program tell us that we will experience the
restoration of meaning and purpose, and we will feel
like full-fledged human beings again. Now we are finding those promises coming true every day. There is always plenty to be depressed about. However, we have
something to do, we have the love of others, and we
have hope for our future.

*Today my gratitude and purpose carry me along with
plenty to be happy about.*

Can you accept the idea that some things happen for no reason, that there is randomness in the universe?

—Rabbi Harold S. Kushner

Whenever something bad happens to us, we ask, *why?* We want to make sense out of our misfortune. *How could this happen to me? Why do I have to suffer this tragedy?* Sometimes we even explain our pain by saying we deserve it for being bad. It is true that many bad things have happened because of bad choices we made. But many things happen for no reason. Illness, death, and pain come into every life. There is no reasonable explanation except that these things are random.

So we accept that fact. We take reasonable precautions, drive carefully, and take our vitamins. Most of all, we hold close to our human connections because we are all in this together. The comforting bonds of trusted friends and loved ones form the human net that holds us up through tough challenges. Within our human network, we celebrate our good times, we play and take joy in life, and we support each other when we need it.

Today I will go beyond the question why? *and hold close to the life-giving bonds of human love.*

> *Man's real home is not a house but the road, and life*
> *itself is a journey to be walked on foot.*
>
> —Bruce Chatwin

We often say that one of our main needs in life is security. We want to be able to predict and control how things will play out. The problem with this view is that even when we gain more control, it doesn't generally make us feel deeply secure. If we accept security as our goal, we are soon on an endless search for more. A much wiser goal is to walk the road of life, accepting that it is always insecure. Happiness isn't found by pursuing happiness, and a sense of security isn't found by grasping for more security. They are both found by indirect means.

We find security by making peace with our insecurity and by trusting our Higher Power to care for our lives. We find happiness by taking on work that has meaning beyond ourselves.

> *Today I will walk on foot the journey that has meaning*
> *and value and accept the insecure feelings that are*
> *part of life.*

*Until you make peace with who you are, you'll never
be content with what you have.*

—Doris Mortman

Marketers call us consumers. Television commercials
suggest that a new car will make us happy or that
when we buy our special loved one a beautiful dia-
mond, we will really be somebody. But our awakening
into a healthy, new life has nothing to do with what
we own. Sure, it's fun to buy something new, but it
doesn't make us happy for long. We don't define ourselves as mere consumers; rather, we are men with
meaning in our lives.

When we haven't got ourselves on track, when we
don't have a focus for our lives, we are easily seduced by
distractions and dead-end promises. Peace of mind
hasn't come easily for most of us. We had to accept
some things about ourselves that we didn't want to accept. We had to learn some lessons that we couldn't
easily learn at first. Now we feel like real men. We have
something much better than anything we could buy
with money, and no one else can take it away.

*Today and every day I restore my peace of mind by
making peace with myself.*

February

To ease another's heartache is to forget one's own.

—Abraham Lincoln

Sometimes, in our self-centeredness, we fall into a pit of self-pity. Most of us have enough pain and heartache to feed a lifetime of self-pity if we choose to. We all have had serious losses, stressful jobs, difficult family relationships, bad breaks, and unfair dealings with others. When we start to sink into excessive self-absorption and resentment or wallow in endless negativity, we may not even recognize what we are doing. The best way to climb out of this pit is to reach out to help others who have real needs.

We can volunteer at a school to help children learn to read, or visit people in nursing homes, or help clean up a riverbank, or help a disabled person buy groceries. When we focus too much on ourselves, we become narrow and negative, but when we bring help or relief to our community, we become connected and we have a purpose and a mission that expands our world.

Today I will reach out to others with a helpful hand.

In marriage, being the right person is as important as finding the right person.

—Wilbert Donald Gough

No matter how much two people love each other, no matter how compatible they are, no matter how great they are as lovers, they will confront matters and situations where their habits and differences will clash. When we face a frustrating obstacle, our first impulse is to blame the other person who doesn't fit what we want. However, our most effective way of improving our relationship is to look beyond that first impulse and focus on what we can change: ourselves. We need to persistently be the best partner we know how to be. Our partner is not a model of our own creation and was not put on this earth just to fulfill our own image.

As good partners we try to be good listeners and open ourselves to our beloved. We cut our partner some slack when it's needed; we offer forgiveness. We don't use our partner's immature response as an excuse for us to be immature. We practice the kind of detachment that allows our partner self-determination. We don't try to fix or mold our beloved to our wishes.

Today I will focus on being the best partner I know how to be, regardless of what my partner says or does.

*You don't get harmony when everybody sings the
same note.*

—Doug Floyd

A tradition of our healing program is that we put principles above personalities. When we encounter a di-
verse group of people, we find some with whom we feel
an immediate affinity and closeness, and others we
don't particularly like. But we can learn something
valuable from both types. Whether at our workplace,
at our place of worship, or in our Twelve Step meetings, the diversity of a group enriches everyone. The
wisdom of two or three is greater than the closed loop
in our own individual mind.

Sometimes it takes awhile to arrive at that wisdom.
The Twelve Steps were created by a group of people trying to formulate a set of suggestions that they had
found effective as a path of recovery. They disagreed
and debated over how to express that set of steps.
What they created was better than what any one of
them could have done alone. The groups we are in have
the same spiritual creative process working for our
own recovery. So we listen to the harmony created by
the wisdom of our group. Even when we don't like
what we hear, we continue the dialogue and we grow
through it.

*Today I am grateful for the harmony created by the
diversity of people in my life.*

An ounce of apology is worth a pound of loneliness.

—Joseph Joubert

The healing that comes when we make amends happens in two places. First of all, it mends the split between what we want to be and the mistake we have made. In that way, we take responsibility for our actions and reaffirm our standards for ourselves. It's a way of respecting ourselves by saying, I believe in the standard that I didn't keep and I will try harder next time.

The second place that healing may happen is between ourself and the person we have harmed. If it's an old mistake, with apology long overdue, the relationship may take on renewed meaning after an apology. It opens the possibility for a discussion about the friendship and its importance to each person. In other situations, an apology doesn't heal the connection and perhaps the other person isn't willing to accept it. In such a situation, we still take comfort in knowing that we have restored the split within ourselves and we can let go of the past.

Today I will be sincere and quick with my apologies.

I never think of the future, it comes soon enough.

—Albert Einstein

In our spiritual development, we learn to think about time in new ways. Many of us have come to our healing journey stuck in the past, imprisoned by fears or angers that arose years ago. We live in the past through regrets and griefs about things that can never change, and we translate them into the future with fears and foreboding. Yet we all know that life is only in the present. All we need to do is live today.

Our memories shaped us but our development is not finished. Today, we don't have to deal with all the problems we can foresee in the future. Today we are given a hand to play, and we can play the cards we have as we choose. With the spiritual guidance of our recovery path, we can resolve the pain of the past and our fears of the future. Our Higher Power reassures us that we will never be alone.

Today, once again, I awake into the present and I thank God for the chance to live this day. I will let my Higher Power care for my fears and regrets.

Real friends are those who, when you've made a fool of yourself, don't feel that you've done a permanent job.

—Erwin T. Randall

Friendship is one of the most important elements in a rich and joyful life. Good mental health requires that we not walk through life without one or two good friends. Many of us have been very lonely. We built invisible shields around ourselves that protected us from letting others know what we were thinking or doing, but they also separated us from the comfortable closeness of good friends. Many of us have a deep and abiding anxiety about being vulnerable to anyone, and many of us are especially guarded about getting close to other men.

In our growth as men, we are abandoning notions of perfection in ourselves and in others. We don't expect perfection, and we can expect our friends to cut us some slack when they see our mistakes and our weaknesses. True friends see in each other a complex weaving of many qualities, many experiences, and a mixture of more and less attractive qualities.

Today I will give my friendships the primary place they deserve.

Time spent laughing is time spent with the gods.

                       —Japanese proverb

Many of our stories have both a dark and a light side. As we make peace with ourselves, we can take ourselves less seriously. We hang out with others who have had similar experiences and we begin to relax. That is when the healing effect of laughter can move in. The worst of times has its funny side, and learning to laugh at it lightens the burden.

The inside jokes of a group that has lived through hard times are wonderful things to share. Suddenly we don't feel so alone. If my brother can laugh at the stupid things he did, I can laugh at myself too. That sense of recognition—we know what it was like, we are insiders—is another form of bonding that heals us.

Today I will not take myself so seriously that I cannot laugh at myself.

Growing old is not growing up.

—Doug Horton

We have all met men who seemed very wise and strong for their age and other men who seemed immature and stuck in a boyish mind with an aging body. So we ask, what is a truly grown-up man? We think of masculine values we admire, such as strength, courage, the ability to think for oneself, wisdom, self-respect, and a sense of balance and proportion in one's actions and relationships.

Many of us have felt that we never really grasped the key to what adult masculinity was all about. We could play the role, and we could make it look pretty good, but we didn't feel in our hearts that it was ours. By walking the daily path in which we get to know ourselves from the inside, and by learning to stay true to ourselves, we develop a true self. Our true self is, by definition, no longer trapped in boyhood. We have found our inner gyroscope, and from that comes the sterling feeling of authenticity that we wouldn't trade for anything.

Today I am grateful for the wisdom and strength of character that is growing within.

I'm more like I am now than I ever was before.

—Anonymous

We are becoming more ourselves. That is our true calling. If we grow wiser and stronger with life experience, we learn to know ourselves and we find the confidence and courage to fulfill our best self. We walk a path that is sometimes very difficult and complicated. Weighing the choices before us, we seldom have a clear, unequivocal answer. But as we know ourselves better and as we gain confidence, we gradually fulfill our true nature.

A story in the *Talmud* describes a man at the end of his life who fears that he will be judged by God for not living a life like Moses. The rabbi replies that God will not judge him for not being Moses, but for not being himself.

Today I will allow myself to be more like I am than I ever did before.

All our loves are first loves.

—Susan Fromberg Schaeffer

When we fall in love with someone, it is a unique thing that comes from deep within us. Any relationship is the creation of two people who open themselves to each other and share themselves beyond the usual boundaries. That is the excitement of true love. Two people give each other the keys to their private world, just as we might share the key to our home, trusting that it will be used with care and respect. This intimacy isn't usually instantaneous. It builds on experience together.

In an intimate relationship, we have the responsibility to be good stewards of the trust given to us. Looking at our partner's role is always so much easier than looking at our own, but we need to resist that easy temptation. Our first questions should always be, Do I make it safe for my partner to be open with me? Do I take my partner's vulnerability as a trust that I do not abuse? Am I gentle and respectful with the key my partner gave me?

Today I will be a good partner, honoring and guarding the trust I have been given.

I imagine that God speaks to me, saying simply, "I kept calling to you, and you did not come." And I answer quite naturally, "I couldn't until I knew there was nowhere else to go."

—Florida Scott-Maxwell

We are willful. We worship individual determination and guts. A man wants to do things in the way that he devises for himself, and it may not occur to him to open himself up to a Higher Power. Yet our Higher Power is always there, calling to us.

There is a paradox in this spiritual lesson: more genuine strength and more options are in our hands when we let go of our willful, controlling attitudes. This is the secret wisdom of a man who has learned from experience. The young, unseasoned man tries to control everything and push on things that he cannot budge. The wiser, more experienced man says, "I see the limits of what is mine to change, and I can let my Higher Power take care of the things I cannot change."

Today I will notice those concerns that I cannot fix, and I will let them go. Then I will focus on a few areas where I can make a difference.

All life is an experiment.

—Ralph Waldo Emerson

When we take a trip, we make many plans and reservations. We have expectations for what we will see, whom we will visit, and what we will do. But the real purpose of a trip is to experience what happens while we follow our plans. We leave our routine of controlled and predictable days to enter another space where we will find novelty and the unpredictable. In fact, our whole life, from beginning to end, is a trip.

Once we accept that much of life is outside of our control, we can step aside. We make plans and work toward our highest goals. We take great pleasure in working toward our achievements. At the same time, the substance of life is not in controlling the outcomes but in responding to what happens along the way.

Today I will be open and respond to what happens while I follow my plans.

There is a basket of fresh bread on your head, and yet you go door to door asking for crusts.

—Rumi

We have often tried to satisfy a deep inner hunger that we could not describe and didn't understand. We followed the seductive call of sexual pleasures, the allure of alcohol or drugs, the excitement of gambling, or even the satisfactions of being the helpful codependent hero, saving others from their problems. These hollow attractions never satisfied our hunger. No matter how much we tried, they only left us more trapped in a dead-end search and less satisfied than ever.

We find genuine satisfactions for our hunger when we develop self-respect, form caring bonds with friends, develop relationship with our Higher Power, and follow a path with heart. All of that is available to us and we only need to turn toward it to find it.

Today I seek a real slice of satisfaction in life rather than settling for crumbs.

All shall be well, and all shall be well, and all manner of things shall be well.

—Julian of Norwich

Some mornings we wake with anxiety, fretting over the future or the state of our lives. Not many things we do will change the direction of events in the future. Our fears for our safety and well-being may be based more on habit than reality, and our desires for control only feed frustration.

To restore calm we can turn to the care of our Higher Power. We do that in our deep meditation, taking a few minutes alone in a quiet, undisturbed, and safe place. We can breathe slowly and deeply, allowing the chair or the floor to hold our body as we allow our Higher Power to hold us. Repeating in our minds today's opening quote, we find calm settling over us.

Today I accept that all will be well.

Take your work seriously but yourself lightly.

—C. W. Metcalf

As we found comfort in our addiction and codependency, we created great problems and chaos in our lives. We come into recovery with a sense of relief that we are no longer living from crisis to crisis, but we still have to deal with our persistent longing for control and security. Many of us get drawn into the same search for comfort by overindulging in work. Work can become another addictive escape from developing as spiritual men with deep emotional lives.

Perhaps a long-standing insecurity about our place at work keeps us working longer hours than necessary, taking few vacations, or even working seven days a week. Perhaps a deep feeling of guilt and shame drives us into unending work, as if we could redeem ourselves by working harder and longer. No matter how virtuous or successful we are at work, it will only cover these underlying fears, never resolve them. Only by facing our insecurities and guilts directly will we ever grow spiritually.

Today I will take time to play, to spend time in my relationships, and perhaps just to loaf.

*We must learn to reawaken and keep ourselves awake,
not by mechanical aids, but by an infinite expectation
of the dawn.*

—Henry David Thoreau

The wisdom of hope in the face of trouble is a fundamental principle of the spiritual path. We expect to have problems, and we have already come through many of them. Our hopes aren't dashed by them. Our awakening in the spiritual life means that even in the darkest night, we can have an infinite expectation that dawn always comes. We have problems, we respond to them, and things get better.

Our spirituality shows us how to have serenity in the face of risk. We accept the darkness because it is inevitable, but we are not defeated by it. We rise above it with our trust in our Higher Power to lead us toward the inevitable light.

*Today my awakening means I trust in a Higher Power
to lead me to a better future.*

Feeling gratitude and not expressing it is like wrapping a present and not giving it.

—William Arthur Ward

We could never have arrived at this point in our lives without the help of a lot of other people. It has been said that we stand on the shoulders of all those who have gone before us. But we also benefited from many people in our lives who were kind, who believed in us when we didn't believe very strongly in ourselves—and from the anonymous multitude of men and women who shone a light on the path to recovery. Sometimes we know within our hearts that someone made a big difference to us, but it is hard to admit it to that person. We may even develop a grudging attitude toward people who have helped us because we are stingy about giving them any credit.

The surprising thing about gratitude is that the more we express it, the larger it grows. As grown men, we all have a mountain of things and people to be thankful for. If we don't express gratitude, our withholding diminishes us. The more we say it and give it away, the bigger and stronger we feel.

Today I will thank someone who has helped me.

*If you do not make it empty, how will you fill it
up again?*

—Neem Karoli Baba

There is a myth that most men believe: we should always be on top of any situation, and we shouldn't show
weakness or vulnerability. But the myth creates a paradox, because if we are never vulnerable, we are never
open to learning anything new. How can we learn anything new if we have to look like we already know the
answers? So we become weaker while trying to appear
strong.

It is said that nothing can be added to a vessel that is
already full. A truly strong, wise man is willing to
doubt, and willing to empty himself of his preconceived
ideas so that he continues to learn and grow.

*Today I will not concern myself with being right.
Instead I will strive to have an open mind.*

Conscience is God's presence in man.

—Emanuel Swedenborg

As we mature, our conscience grows, and vice versa. We follow a principle that directs us to promptly admit when we are wrong. That practical piece of guidance is the most effective way to become bigger, stronger men. To follow it, we must abandon our ego's desire to always be right. We must abandon the thought that we are belittled by such an admission.

In this process of becoming better men, we open ourselves and allow God to enter. We let God speak to us and through us by humbly accepting that we don't always have to be right. The higher principles of honesty and responsibility are our guides, and we don't expect perfection from ourselves. In that way, we become more honest with ourselves and with our friends.

Today I will be open to the truth that my Higher Power speaks within me.

Woe to the man so possessed that he possesses God!

　　　　　　　　　　　　　—Martin Buber

When we first set out on this spiritual path, we learn that a relationship with "God as we understood Him" is a requirement for healing. So many of us think that we have to begin by defining our personal understanding of God. This is indeed a good question for us to think about. Yet the greatest thinkers, beginning in the most ancient times, have told us that God is truly beyond definition. In the oldest Judeo-Christian history, even the name of God could not be pronounced.

It is one thing to ask where we find our spiritual renewal. It is another thing to try to invent it. And as soon as we think we have the answer, as soon as we believe we hold the true definition of God, we may be off the spiritual path. In the end, the true spiritual path is always a learning process and has a good deal of mystery.

Today I turn my life over to God, Whom I can never fully understand.

Why not go out on a limb? Isn't that where the fruit is?

—Frank Scully

From the day we are born, our lives are risky. We may be intimidated by a task or a challenge before us. Working on some of the Twelve Steps is a risk. When we face these challenges, we can draw courage from looking at other risks we have taken and perhaps even enjoyed. For instance, most sports are exciting and thrilling because they play on the possibility of winning or losing. Falling in love is a risk. Climbing a mountain is a risk. Building something with our hands is a risk. Yet we enjoy the pleasure of stepping into these risks. Taking a risk makes us feel alive.

When we think about these enjoyable adventures, where risks add to the excitement, we can use that feeling as a model for approaching the risks that we avoid. Perhaps we need to talk to our wife or partner about something that is hard to say. Perhaps we need to make amends to someone for a past wrong and we don't know how we will be received. Perhaps our greatest challenge is to subdue our own will for something and give it over to the care of our Higher Power.

Today I will recall the risks that make me feel alive and move forward with those things I have been avoiding.

To remain whole, be twisted. To become straight, let yourself be bent. To become full, be hollow.

—Lao Tzu

The first three Steps of our Twelve Step program make the ancient spiritual wisdom real in our lives. First we give in to the fact that we are powerless in a very real way in our lives. Then we open ourselves to the healing that comes not of our own making but from our Higher Power.

We live the paradox of spiritual development. Every day that we admit the ways in which we are powerless, and every day that we live in true humility, we become stronger, wiser men. Although we aren't totally powerless, there are some things we can never control. Owning up to that truth makes us stronger. Having the respect that is inherent in humility makes us grow in wisdom.

Today I am grateful for the spiritual guidance I am learning in this program.

You may be disappointed if you fail, but you are doomed if you don't try.

—Beverly Sills

Anyone who has achieved great things has also faced failure. Learning how to deal with disappointment and loss is a first step in moving forward in life. We cannot live happily and well if we have not learned how to handle failure. Some of us were traumatized by terrible events in our past and reacted by seeking only security and control. Some of us were so ashamed and guilty about our out-of-control addiction and codependency that in recovery we have avoided all risk.

On the healing path we strive to be calm even though disappointment is possible. We can cope because our self-esteem doesn't have to be at risk. We can feel good about ourselves when we go up to bat and give our best swing, even if we strike out. We may have tried to avoid losses by staying out of the game completely. But when we join the game and play our best, we feel better about ourselves; we enjoy life more and continue to grow. That is the only way we will find the joy of success.

Today I will step up to bat and give life my best swing.

*No man who sets out to achieve total masculinity can
ever be man enough.*

—Frank Pittman

Some people attack the whole idea of masculinity as a
problem in the world. They claim it is the cause of wars,
abuse, and the reckless pursuit of power. As grown-up
men, we know that those people are speaking of masculinity that has not grown up. Boys trying to be men
take the appearance of masculinity to extremes. They
look at masculinity from the outside: they know they
have not yet achieved it, so they try to imitate it. As
adult men we have come to terms with ourselves and
with life. We carry the values of strength and protection of those we love, and we value our virility for all its
pleasures. We also know from life experience that all
men are complex; we don't need to hide our vulnerability in order to be strong.

We don't have to worry about our masculinity, because that is a given. We don't have to prove it to ourselves or anyone else. From that grown-up perspective,
we accept ourselves as both strong and gentle, capable
both of fighting for what we believe in and yielding to
others when that's what's called for.

*Today I accept that I have nothing to prove about being
a man, and I can grow in all the ways any adult needs
to continue to grow.*

It is only with the heart that one can see rightly; what is essential is invisible to the eye.

—Antoine de Saint-Exupéry

We are surrounded by cynical attitudes and mistrust. We carry large rings of keys that symbolize all the guards we maintain as part of ordinary daily life. It is hard for us to develop a vision from our hearts amidst all this wariness. Indeed, we are trying to move beyond the scorn and contempt of the mainstream world. What we pursue is an alternative and wiser way.

What the heart can see is the deeper man in the person next to us. Sometimes, with our hearts, we see good as well as bad inside ourselves and others. We can see a future developing for our children and all the little people around us. Instead of protecting only ourselves, we also see opportunities to help others and to take on worthwhile projects that benefit our communities; we escape the narrow confines of our self-centeredness. With exercise, our vision grows stronger every day and we see more.

Today I will open my heart to see beyond my personal walls and into the true nature of those around me.

March

Every man I meet is in some way my superior.

—Ralph Waldo Emerson

When we are in a competitive frame of mind, we compare ourselves to those around us. We may conclude that we are better in some ways and worse in other ways. Perhaps the smallest part of our personality takes a dark pleasure in looking down on others. Some of us feel inferior to almost everyone.

The true measure of a man has many dimensions. Is he physically strong, mentally determined, generous, a good father, a good partner, courageous, honest, wise, warm-hearted, responsible for himself, intelligent, musically talented, athletically gifted, a good communicator? Good qualities are countless. No one has all of them—and sometimes too much of a good thing is a bad thing. When we reach the place where we accept ourselves and make peace with who we are, we can comfortably accept everyone else, knowing that their strengths and weaknesses add up in different ways, and everyone deserves basic human respect.

Today I will practice respect for everyone I meet.

I visualize the course nine or ten times every night as I'm going to sleep. By race day, I've run the course a hundred times in my head.

—A. J. Kitt, Olympic skier

A world-class athlete reaches the pinnacle of performance by intense work and dedication. No one doubts his priorities. He practices for hours every day, endures the pain of pushing his body to the limit, and develops his mind psychologically to be ready to respond in a split second. We can use that same model for our healing recovery program. We need to put our recovery above all else—because without that, we have nothing. We need to accept the pain that comes with facing ourselves and our truth, because on the other side of the pain is peace of mind. And we can develop our self-image as recovering men in the care of our Higher Power, succeeding as we meet the challenges of our days.

A very helpful daily practice is to visualize ourselves in a quiet place, feeling well, content, and safe. Staying with this image for fifteen minutes or so, just enjoying its peace, creates a sense of strength and serenity for the next few hours or for the rest of the day.

Today I know my first priority is recovery and I can picture myself feeling content in a quiet setting.

*Love is an ideal thing, marriage is a real thing;
a confusion of the real with the ideal never goes
unpunished.*

—Johann Wolfgang von Goethe

Everybody knows about the adjustment required by
two people when they decide to become life partners.
Part of that adjustment is moving from feelings of
pleasure and excitement to managing the more practical aspects of daily life. In that interdependent life, we
have to carry our share of the work. Sometimes we may
feel let down; sometimes our partner will feel let down
by us. We have to deal with differing sexual appetites
and learn how to respect the differences while maintaining the connection.

The practical is never as heavenly as the ideal. When
we enter the realm of life partnership, while we may
struggle and feel confused or frustrated at times, we
come to know each other more deeply—and we become
more vulnerable. Our first task is to be sure that our
partner, while vulnerable in deep and real ways, is in
good hands with us. That means we don't willingly
hurt our partner and we don't use abusive or threaten-
ing words. At the same time, we expect our own vulnerability and trust will be handled with care by our
partner. When these ground rules are in place and followed, our intimacy continues to deepen through the
practical details of our lives.

*Today I accept the real world of daily life in my
love life.*

*Great opportunities to help others seldom come, but
small ones surround us every day.*

—Sally Koch

From its earliest days, the Twelve Step program began
with the Twelfth Step. When the first recovering man
in Ohio was tentatively making his way into sobriety,
day by day, he quickly realized that his progress de-
pended upon telling his story to other suffering alcoholics. He realized that by helping others, he was
helping himself stay sober.

A fundamental rule of good mental health is to be
helpful to others. We can do that by telling our story:
where we were and how far we have come. But helpful-
ness is an attitude. We can cultivate this attitude, looking for ways to be helpful while not taking on a
caretaking role. Generosity of spirit in all our dealings
with others, without looking for anything in return,
creates a feeling of connection with others. Helping
others can also dispel depression and self-pity.

*Today I will look for ways to be helpful and generous
to others.*

I just keep goin' up there and swingin' at 'em.

—Babe Ruth

Even Babe Ruth had his share of strikeouts. On this recovery path, relapse is always a possibility, and we need to learn how to avoid it—and how to deal with it if it happens. What do many guys feel first when they relapse? Shame. This feeling may be unavoidable, but we do best if we don't stay there long. It is not what we deserve to feel, and it weakens us rather than strengthens us. After a relapse, the first productive thing to do is tell our recovery group and our sponsor. When we do that, we expose our addictive and codependent side. That side may want to stay hidden and secret, but our recovery requires that we shine the light of day on it.

The second thing to do is ask ourselves what we can learn from this relapse. If we can learn the lessons it has to teach us, it is no longer a deficit but an asset that strengthens our healing. Some relapses happen when we fail to take care of ourselves; we get too worn out, too depleted, too needy. Some happen because we associate with others who support our addictive impulses rather than with those who have our best interests at heart. The bottom line is that a relapse occurs because we are addicts and codependent. After a strikeout we can still go up there and swing at 'em again.

Today I know once again that I am powerless over my addiction and my codependency.

Listen, or thy tongue will keep thee deaf.

—Native American proverb

Much of what we learn on this path comes from others also making their way. We go to meetings and listen to their reflections and their stories and we say, *that's like me.* When neighbors or friends at work tell us about their lives, we often gain insight about our own. Sometimes we think, *I guess I didn't have it so bad.* By being a good listener, we may get encouragement to stay on the path.

It's an honor to have others disclose to us what they have been through. And it's a trust that we ought to respect. Listening with an open heart isn't always easy. It doesn't mean that we simply sit there while others talk. It means that we engage actively to perceive what they are telling us and to understand how they came to feel and think as they do. When we put our ego aside, we stop thinking about what we will say in response; we stop trying to offer helpful advice or a better answer. We just take in what they are trying to tell us.

Today I will actively engage as a good listener.

One has to go beyond the pairs of opposites to find the real source.

—Joseph Campbell

We have the habit of seeing things in absolute terms, as either black or white, all or nothing, good or evil. Perhaps we find comfort in the simplicity of a clear and total answer. But this habit leads us down many mistaken paths. We might think, *since I made a mistake I must be a bad person.* Or perhaps, *after he insulted me, I can never be his friend.*

Rarely do we find truth at the extremes. Within our complex human nature we must deal with many different drives and forces. We feel generous and giving, and we feel selfish. We want to be helpful and caring, but sometimes we get so angry we feel like hurting someone. When we can accept the mixture of drives within ourselves, we can learn to manage them as good and mature men. Sometimes we need to make repairs after we break our own rules. Sometimes we say something that we regret, and we need to stay in the dialogue to reach a new understanding. When we can accept our own complexity, we become much more understanding of the same in others.

Today I will look for the middle ground between extremes.

To be without some of the things you want is an
indispensable part of happiness.

—Bertrand Russell

We learn, as we make peace with ourselves, that we have enough. Our old mind became anxious if we thought we needed something we could not have. We feared we would not be safe or comfortable, and we sought security in the comfort of things. Like the rush to the food market before a storm, the prospect of scarcity haunted us and we got anxious.

On the spiritual path we learn to say, "I have enough. I will not have more to deal with than I can handle. All will be well. I am in the care of my Higher Power." We can't say it once and have it settled. Just as we practice safe driving or healthy eating habits, this is called spiritual practice because we continue doing it. We often forget the reassurance and we need to keep returning to it. Something changes inside when we accept that we can be at peace, and we can be happy, even when we don't have everything we want.

Today I live with satisfaction that I have enough.

Courage doesn't always roar. Sometimes courage is that little voice at the end of the day that says: "I'll try again tomorrow."

—Anne Hunninghake

A key quality that distinguishes a successful athlete, or a top-notch performer in any field, is the way he responds to his bad days. Everyone has good days and bad days, and the good ones are certainly easier to handle. But do we allow the bad ones to throw us off our course? Are we so shaken by our mistakes or troubles that we lose our focus on our goals?

Adult development is a process; it's never an end goal that we reach and hold. Our healing and recovery includes preparing ourselves to respond well to the bad days. We can do that by keeping our eye on the big picture, knowing that however bad things may seem at the moment, they will change. We learn to reach deep into our spiritual center for the courage to stay focused in the midst of our hardest days. We don't have to do it alone. We have the spiritual support of our Higher Power and the companionship of our friends to keep us on the path.

Today I will stay in touch with my spiritual center to find the courage for another day.

*At the heart of the simple life is an emphasis on
harmonious and purposeful living.*

—Duane Elgin

At some point, we all complain about the fast pace and
complexity of modern life. We rush the kids to school
or day care, and when we get to work, we practice multitasking, trying to be more efficient and productive.
Driving home from work, we catch up on some phone
calls. But somehow, as busy as we are, we are never led
to that point of completion with calm and quiet—only
to more busyness.

To have a simpler life, we have to consciously choose
it. Busily running around and embracing more tasks
does not open the door to simplicity. We can decide
not to be frantic and scattered in our daily tasks.
Instead we can be attentive, present in the moment,
and focused on the one thing that is before us. Being in
harmony with our surroundings is at least as important as efficiency. When we choose to push back against
the hectic pace and move toward simplicity and harmony, we think more clearly, we know ourselves better,
we make better choices, our physical health is stronger,
and maybe we are actually more productive.

Today I will choose simplicity and harmony.

*Never believe that a few caring people can't change the
world, for indeed, that's all who ever have.*

—Margaret Mead

The pessimists and the naysayers believe that the future is bleak. Storm clouds are always present somewhere, they say, leading things inexorably to the worse. Yet our own recovery and our restored lives are living proof that growth and improvement are always possible. We know how bad things felt in our own lives and how much better they have now become. Our own experience is all we need to give us hope.

When a couple of guys in Ohio first got together to find a path out of alcoholism and despair, they started a Twelve Step recovery program that has brought hope and transformation to millions. When so many around them were hopelessly caught in the grip of alcoholism, these guys dared to hope that they could be restored to sanity. They changed the world.

On this day, perhaps we see danger looming. We may despair about a relationship, or worry about a friend or loved one. But if we care, and if we keep the faith, we know that things can change for the better.

*Today I will carry the knowledge that a Power greater
than ourselves can restore us.*

Fear will assault us, but we will not be afraid.

—Rabbi Harold S. Kushner

Worry and concern are among our biggest challenges as we follow our paths. Nothing can finally and completely shield us from the vulnerabilities and unknowns. We may be haunted by experiences from our past when our safety and security were stripped away. In the back of our minds, we carry images of chaotic moments. Now we are seeking something called peace of mind and serenity—but we have to find a way to do that in the face of universal insecurity.

Many of us feel innocent about our controlling behavior because we think we are only trying to make everyone safe and secure. The practice of a good life requires us to learn attitudes and understandings that help us let go of fear when it assaults us. This means that we turn to our spiritual foundation, knowing that we are never alone and that even though we cannot control everything, the forces of a Power greater than ourselves also move in our best interest. We can quiet our minds by cultivating a close relationship with our Higher Power.

Today I will walk my path, knowing that my Higher Power is beside me.

Being defeated is often a temporary condition. Giving up is what makes it permanent.

—Marilyn vos Savant

Powerlessness and helplessness are two very different things. When we encounter something we cannot change and we pray to accept its truth, we gain the wisdom of powerlessness. The new reality that follows acceptance may transform us or teach us a new lesson.

Sometimes, however, we encounter something that can be changed, yet the challenge seems overwhelming. It's natural to feel intimidated when facing a high mountain before us. We feel like running away or pretending it isn't there, or we just want to lie down and give up. When we actually give in to those feelings and hide from the hard task, we choose helplessness, and nothing gets better.

Challenges rise up in everyone's path. So we look squarely into the eye of the challenge before us today. We get to know its dimensions as well as we can see them. It may seem either daunting or small. We can choose to take one specific action that will move us a little closer to our goal. Just one small action keeps us from the condition of helplessness, of giving up.

Today I will do what I can in this one day, and it will be progress.

*He knows not his own strength that hath not met
adversity.*

—Ben Jonson

A man who has never had difficult times, lived through
the pain of loss, or confronted a big mistake has nothing to fall back on. In getting through our hard times
we learn to know ourselves better. We find our strong
sides and our weaknesses. And in the end, as difficult
as some adversity can be, we have survived—and survival itself is a good thing.

Some of us are in the midst of difficult times today.
From this spot we may not be able to see where the
road leads next. We are fearful about how things will
turn out. In the spiritual life, we accept that we cannot
know where this path leads, or even what is around the
next bend, but we never have to be alone. Because we
will stay true to ourselves and do what is honest and
fair, we can take risks to make things better.

*Today I will rely on my Higher Power and my friends
as my guide through difficult times.*

I imagine one of the reasons people cling to their hates so stubbornly is because they sense, once hate is gone, they will be forced to deal with pain.

—James Baldwin

Why do we hold on to our resentments and our hates? They poison our personality and keep us in a negative state of mind. Maybe some of us don't know any better or don't realize we have any other options. Probably some of us don't want to face the feelings we have underneath. Hate and resentment are secondary emotions. They cover more primary feelings such as hurt, grief, emptiness, and low self-worth.

So we face our true feelings and let go of hate and resentment. This is painful at first. Our egos want to hold onto the protection, claiming we are entitled to feel so negative. We justify these feelings, but they only keep us stuck. When we get honest with ourselves about our underlying feelings, we can start changing what we can change. Our burden is lightened and we are free to move on with our lives.

Today I will face my primary feelings and let go of my negativity.

Human beings love to be right. When a person is willing to give up being right, a whole world of possibilities opens up.

—Pete Salmansohn

We naturally want others to respect us. Our urge to be right, even when we are wrong, gets us into many jams. We have seen others laughed at for their mistakes, and we ourselves have done some of the laughing. Maybe we have been the target of ridicule for not knowing the right answer or the right way to do something.

A grown-up man has lived enough and seen enough to know that honest mistakes are inevitable; indeed, they are lessons. In fact, the only way we learn is by trying out an idea, testing a new method. When we are open to seeing reality as it is, rather than blindly defending our rightness, we get wiser.

As grown men, we voice our ideas honestly, and we listen to others. We don't have to push our ideas as right. We can take on the attitude of dignity and open-mindedness, seeking the best answer and always learning.

Today I will consciously set aside my drive to always be right so that I can continue to learn.

A "no" uttered from the deepest conviction is better and greater than a "yes" merely uttered to please, or what is worse, to avoid trouble.

—Mahatma Gandhi

We don't like to make anyone unhappy with us. We don't like to hurt anyone's feelings. We feel best when others tell us they like what we do. And we have the idea that we are strong enough to put aside our own wishes and feelings when others have strong desires. In our denial we tell ourselves, "I can handle it." We have even violated our sense of what is right because someone else insisted.

Many a man has gotten himself into serious problems because he didn't muster the courage to say no at critical times. In sexual situations we said, "I couldn't hurt her feelings." In work situations we said, "I am only doing it the way everyone else does it." Within our families we said, "I don't want to cause an uproar." But now, with our good values and our good intuition, we can find the strength to stand up for what we believe. We have our honor and our self-respect for staying honest.

Today I will speak my honest truth, not to be right but to be true to myself.

Who forces time is pushed back by time; who yields to time finds time on his side.

—The *Talmud*

We are impatient for results. Upon entering a program of recovery, going without a drink or giving up other addictive behaviors for more than a day or a week seems like a huge challenge. When we see friends in recovery with several years of sobriety, we can't imagine achieving that. Future time can seem like a mountain. Our attitude shifts when we see time not as a challenge that we must overcome, but as our friend, working for us. Time is more like a lake that we swim in. It holds us up and carries us along.

One day at a time, we live only in this present moment. We live more fully when we are present to this moment, yielding to what time will do, letting go of frets and worries about the future.

On this day, I will be alive and aware of my experience.

Next time you're feeling at odds with yourself, make a
list of your good qualities . . . things like generosity and
patience and thrift. It will surprise you to discover how
nice you really are.

—Audrey Corn

Some days we just feel out of sorts and down on ourselves. In this program, we place great importance
on self-inventories. We confront our defects and our
wrongs, and we make lists of them to hold ourselves responsible. Any good inventory counts both assets and
liabilities. On a day when we feel burdened with guilt
or weakness, we ought to remind ourselves of the best
of who we are. Remember good deeds that we have
done. Remember what we do well, and don't minimize
those assets. If we are going to build on our strengths,
we have to see them for what they are.

Our attitude toward ourselves and toward life is
partly a matter of mental discipline. It does no good
for anyone if we sit passively in our negativity. We can
learn to affirm that we are children of creation, and we
have a right to be here. In spite of our imperfections,
we are a force for good.

Today I will carry in my thoughts some of my good
qualities.

*We have ever more perfect eyes in a world in which
there is always more to see.*

—Teilhard de Chardin

Today's quotation could be seen as one of the promises
of recovery. When we enter into a program of spiritual
and emotional renewal, we choose to become honest
with ourselves. In the process, our eyes begin to see
more clearly and we become aware of the many ways we
have been dishonest with ourselves. Each new bit of
self-honesty builds the base for more insight and an
ever-sharper understanding of ourselves and our world.
When we started with our decision to be honest, we
could never have predicted what we would find down
the path.

We first surrender to the truth as we know it, and
this clarity about ourselves and the world grows into
great insight. The world opens up for us and we find
ever more to see and learn. We feel very alive every
moment.

*Today I continue my commitment to see the truth
wherever I find it.*

Spring is nature's way of saying, "Let's party!"

—Robin Williams

Our lives are always enriched when we get closer to nature. In springtime, just going for a walk around the block can lift our spirits. Sometimes we feel blue, or we are overwhelmed with emotions that are painful or frightening. Even when our feelings are based on real concerns, we need to manage them in order to confront difficult situations. One of the best things we can do for ourselves is to get outside.

Putting ourselves under the open sky, feeling the weather against our skin, and moving our muscles in a walk or a run changes our emotions and relieves tension. During the worst of times we may have a hard time making ourselves go out and move. But when we do, we always feel better. Spring is nature's promise that nothing is forever. Change and new life are sure to come.

Today I welcome spring as the metaphor that life is constantly being renewed and refreshed.

*If you treat every situation as a life-and-death matter,
you'll die a lot of times.*

—Dean Smith

We have lived through many crises. Many of us grew
up in situations that were chaotic and filled with tur-
moil. We felt constantly on the edge of catastrophe
and needed to be ever-vigilant to avoid it. We lost our
ability to sift and screen what was genuinely in need of
our attention and what we could just turn over to the
work of the universe.

The spiritual part of recovery promises that we can
rest in the care and security of a Higher Power. Not
every situation has to automatically go to the top of
our priority list of things to fix. Even if this is a random universe, forces are always in play to keep things
working and put things in order. Often our anxiety
and our attempts to fix things only get in the way of a
good solution. So we can relax and trust that if we re-
serve our energy for the things we can improve, this
change within ourselves will make the world a better
place.

*Today I will be more discerning about what really is
critical and try to stay out of the way of my Higher
Power.*

Remember that not getting what you want is sometimes a stroke of good luck.

—H. Jackson Brown, Jr.

Managing desires is one of the most crucial elements of being an adult. Children want many things that aren't good for them, and their impulses can often get them into trouble. They need loving, caring adults to protect them from the harm that can come from getting what they want. As adults, our spiritual development includes learning how to regard our desires and how to manage them. On the one hand, it isn't healthy to become so controlled and repressed that we never let ourselves have fun, and on the other hand, we know that indulging every desire will kill us.

Sometimes we want something very badly and when we don't get it, we feel desperate or very disappointed. However, life continuously points us in directions we hadn't expected. Disappointment can serve to reset our lives. Not getting our desires, if we keep our eyes open, points us in directions that can be better than what we had imagined for ourselves.

Today I will be open to the new directions that life points me toward.

Getting angry can sometimes be like leaping into a
wonderfully responsive sports car, gunning the motor,
taking off at high speed and then discovering the brakes
are out of order.

—Maggie Scarf

Anger can multiply our difficulties in many situations.
All of us can look back and remember times when we
only made our problems worse because we stepped on
the gas and lost all ability to use the brakes. Our masculine roles sometimes glorify aggression for its own
sake. We are proud of how aggressive we can be, and we
may confuse it with anger.

Now we are growing into more adult manhood. We
are learning to manage our feelings and use them well.
This doesn't happen overnight. We would do well to
recall how energized we have felt when we let our anger
fly and how much we loved that energy at the moment.
Only later did we face the damage we caused. Saying
we are sorry isn't enough; we must also be willing to
take on the harder task of changing our behavior.
When we accept that we love the power and the energy
of our anger and aggression, we can begin to rein it in
and take charge of it rather than be ruled by it.

Today I will not indulge in the pleasure of anger
allowed to run wild.

My father didn't tell me how to live; he lived, and let me watch him do it.

—Clarence Budington Kelland

The most powerful teaching is done by example. We all have strong feelings about our fathers and what we learned or didn't learn from them. They are as unique to us as our own identity is unique. Some of us have fathers who stand as great examples of how we would like to live. Some of us have fathers who are negative examples that we want to avoid. Some of us feel we never really got to know our fathers. For most of us, it is a complicated mixture of all those things.

Now, as we continue to grow and change in adulthood, we are faced with growing beyond what our parents taught us, both the good and the bad. We need to forge ahead and become our own growing version of adult men. There are many men who can serve as examples to us; some of them were in our past, and some of them are now friends and mentors. Sometimes the example is unconscious. It is always helpful to notice who we admire, who sets an example that we would like to follow. Take the best of what they have to offer and leave the rest.

Today I am grateful for what I received from my father and from all the other men who have set examples in my life.

Tuning and training the mind as an athlete tunes and trains his body is one of the primary aims of all forms of meditation.

—Lawrence LeShan

The longer we follow the steps that guide our path, the more we grow as men. We all know about getting in shape and staying in shape physically. Working out brings results very quickly, and if we are working on our golf game or improving our running time, the more we practice, the more progress we make. We can attend to our minds in the same way. One difference between these kinds of development is that age is on our side as we train our minds. No aging process can diminish the kind of person we are.

Spiritual growth moves forward by paying attention to it and by devoting some time every day to prayer and meditation. Conscious contact with our Higher Power, sitting quietly for a few minutes every day, influences us throughout the day in the background of our minds.

Today I will quietly open my mind to the deep truths and allow them to train my thoughts.

*Somewhere in each of us we're a mixture of light and
of darkness, of love and of hate, of trust and of fear.*

—Jean Vanier

We have gone to extremes in our lives. We've got a pen-
chant for seeing things as all or nothing, black or
white. A real man is made up of mixtures and blends,
but we tend to think of ourselves as either the greatest
or the worst, the smartest or the dullest.

In our progress toward recovery, we see that we are
not separate from other people. We are like all people.
As we learn to know ourselves, we see parts that we
like and parts that appall us. But honesty with ourselves trumps any other defect. So in the very act of admitting a defect, we lay the foundation for accepting
ourselves.

*Today I will be honest with myself about my many
facets and accept the mixture as truly human.*

My history is a gift, like my body—it's what I am made of.

—Shawnee Undell

If our bodies are the hardware, our histories are part of the software. We sometimes cringe when we look back at things we did or things that happened. We are tempted to indulge in magical thinking, hoping to turn back the clock and relive events to make them turn out differently. But our experiences, good and bad, are the stuff that teaches what we need to learn.

When we look back, we cannot change what happened. History is history. But we did choose what we made of what happened, and we can still choose: that is always open to revision. Even today we can deepen and improve upon how we respond to what happened. Our growth continues into the present and for as long as we live.

Today I am responding constructively to what has happened in my history.

The true name of eternity is today.

—Philo

Today is the only focus for our recovery. When we look into the future, we worry. What if I slip when temptations mount at some future time? What if I get lost and confused and fall back into my codependency?

The only real truth is how we live today. The sun will come up tomorrow and we will live the new day as we do this day, in the present moment, staying true to ourselves. Tomorrow's problems are only in our imagination. What are we doing today?

Eternity is beyond time. It is at hand.

Today I am mindful of my immediate moment.

*The last of the human freedoms is to choose one's
attitude in any given set of circumstances.*

—Viktor Frankl

Today's quotation was written by a man who survived
a Nazi death camp. His philosophy was formed in the
crucible of the bleakest kind of situation, in prison
with hard labor, little food, and no comforts, where
everyone was worked until they died. One could say
Frankl had no choices remaining, but he didn't accept
that. He speaks to all of us as we deal with our own
particular circumstances. When we gain the wisdom of
powerlessness, we know that we often have little choice
about what happens, but we have choices about the attitudes we adopt.

When we face a tough situation on the job, we can
still choose to give our best. When family problems
seem overwhelming, we may not be able to fix them all
alone, but we have options to be the best partner, the
best father, or the best son that we know how to be.
And when we turn our lives and our will over to the
care of a Higher Power, we can choose to be hopeful for
the future.

*Today I choose to have a constructive attitude in all
that I am dealing with.*

*Solitude is important to man . . . It is his refuge when
the very foundations of his life are being shaken by
disastrous events.*

—Margaret E. Mular

In modern life, it's much easier to pursue the busy hectic life of work and responsibilities than to pursue solitude. Even though we have often felt very alone, we have been afraid to be alone with ourselves. But it is in those quiet moments alone that we honestly meet ourselves and lay the groundwork to learn from our experiences.

When we are so busy with our intense daily lives, perhaps dealing with crises, and do not take any quiet time for ourselves, we cannot look at where we are going, and we cannot learn from all that experience. Just a few minutes to simply let ourselves breathe is a valuable gem of time set aside that enriches the whole day.

*My quiet moments of solitude are precious elements
in my growing sobriety.*

April

□ □ □ □ □ □ □

> *Be patient toward all that is unsolved in your heart
> and try to love the questions themselves.*
>
> —Rainer Maria Rilke

We carry problems and discrepancies within us, quandaries that are not easily answered—and we have bigger questions about life and the world. Why did I act as I did in my younger years? Can my life partnership be happy again? How should I handle a secret that I carry? What is this thing we call Higher Power and God?

We are on a journey and in some ways, this journey is a quest for answers. The questions give energy and direction to our seeking. We cannot expect to get quick or easy answers. And some questions will always remain just that: questions. But we can learn to be patient with ourselves, tolerant of our incompleteness, and always curious about how it will all turn out.

*Today I will practice patience with myself and embrace
my unsolved questions as crucial elements in my quest.*

*Once the game is over, the king and the pawn go back
into the same box.*

—Italian proverb

We may feel that we are less than other men, or greater
than someone else, but in the big picture we are all created equal. In our low self-esteem, we may feel less worthy than the next guy. Some of us have built defenses
against our shame and guilt by thinking we are superior, but that is still the flip side of the shame coin. No
matter what we have done, no matter what has happened to us, no matter what anyone else says, our behavior and our experiences are not the same as who
we are.

The way to step out of the shame and blame problem with our self-esteem is to accept our humility. The
word *humility* has the same root as *human* and *humus*.
We all are of the earth. Humility is in contrast with hu-
miliation, however. Humility helps us outgrow our
self-absorption and see our connection with all people.
In recovery, no matter what our social status is, we all
deal with addiction and codependency. Our humility
shows us how to be respectful of everyone, including
ourselves.

*Today I accept my humility and equality with all other
people.*

Solitude is the furnace of transformation.

—Henri Nouwen

This path is an alternative to the lifestyles portrayed by Hollywood and the popular media. It is about finding happiness on a deeper level than immediate gratification. It is about a bigger, fuller kind of happiness than we can find in a new car or an erotic one-night stand. No hit TV program shows the way. No commercial touts the joy that can be found in peace of mind.

Solitude is quiet. It is not loneliness and it is not neediness. Solitude is the way we meet ourselves; it is the place where we first get honest and finally accept the truths we have been avoiding. It is the place where we are alone with God. Many of us don't know how to be alone. We have never actually accepted our own companionship or taken on the role of self-care. We can start by taking a few minutes of quiet, in a room or on a park bench. In that quiet moment we might simply make a list of what we are grateful for, or speak to God about what we want help with. In solitude we learn to reach down into our inner well of knowing, where we find guidance.

Today I will seek the solitude that transforms my life.

When you teach your son, you teach your son's son.

—The *Talmud*

As we look at our own life history and begin to understand how we reached this point, we have to examine what was passed on to us by our parents and then realize that they were doing the best they could with what they had been given. We talk about the chain of transmission through generations who had problems with addictions and codependency. Many of us know that we want to break that chain so that our children don't inherit the negative patterns.

How do we break the chain of generation after generation of addiction and abuse? We become the best father we know how to be. We develop genuine relationships with our children, letting them truly know us; we tell them about our lives and listen to them talk about their lives. It isn't all about discipline; it's about having a bond and being honest in telling our children that we love and care for them. Certainly setting limits and being consistent are important tenets, but the most important thing a father can give his child is letting his child know him.

Today I will be engaged with my child in a genuine and open relationship.

In prayer it is better to have a heart without words than words without a heart.

—John Bunyan

Prayer starts with openness in our heart and with self-honesty. We don't sit down to ask special favors from God to achieve our ego's rewards. We quiet our mind. For a brief time we release all the particular details, the worries and tasks that have been rushing in on us. In this quiet space we consciously focus our attention on our relationship with our Higher Power. This is a very private, personal relationship which is known intimately only by us. Even our search for this relationship, even the question, "Where are you, God?" is a prayer.

This healing journey has two aspects. One aspect is fellowship with others, the healing of our separation from our fellow men. The other aspect is a deeply private relationship with our Higher Power. When we have spent some quiet time in prayer, echoes of that prayer stay with us in the back of our mind, no matter how busy and focused we become on our daily tasks.

Today I open my heart with honesty to my Higher Power.

To age with dignity and with courage cuts close to what it is to be a man.

—Roger Kahn

The healing journey requires courage. We are walking a path that is somewhat off the mainstream. We seek to become better men, better friends, better intimate partners, and better fathers. We seek to grow out of our self-centeredness to be more generous and caring. It takes courage to give up the pursuit of greater and greater control, to give up the empty pursuit of happiness through more material possessions. Courage comes forward when we refuse to use our old escapes and accept our problems so we can deal with them.

Nothing is so bad that it can't be talked about. When we choose a trustworthy friend to tell our truth to, we see our situation from new angles. We can then have a dialogue with our friend and within ourselves that leads to a new outlook and new solutions. This kind of connection with other men creates new integrity within ourselves and gives us genuine dignity.

Today I will continue to have courage on my journey of healing.

*Be not forgetful to entertain strangers: for thereby some
have entertained angels unaware.*

—Hebrews 13:2

Recovery is a very democratic thing. No matter how far
down a man has fallen, no matter how bad his life
choices have been or how much he has given up for his
addiction and codependency, he deserves our basic
human respect. We all are created in the image of God.
There is something of God within everyone.

When we go to our meetings, we meet many kinds
of people. Some of them we have more in common
with than others. Some of them we will feel closer to
than others. But we are all creatures of the universe
and we are all equally loved by God. We may feel critical of someone's behavior, but ultimately we are called
to respect everyone as fellow human beings seeking a
path through life.

*Today I accept the love of God and pledge to show
respect to everyone I meet.*

To "be" means to be related.

—Alfred Korzybski

In our using and codependent days, loneliness was ever-present. We could be with a crowd but we felt alienated and alone. Many of us grew up in families where no one really knew how to feel close. We often longed for a closer connection with our fathers. As adult men we learned to be self-sufficient, and we thought it was always superior to be able to do something without help. If we got help to accomplish something, it was somehow not quite as good as if we did it alone.

Now we are part of a fellowship with other men and women who know what it's like to be where we have been; they are on the same journey. We may have very different lives in some ways, but we have our common goal: to become better people. The true basis for our humanity, the real fulfillment of our potential, is in relationship with others. We no longer have to be locked in our isolated world. Through our friendships and our spiritual path we are free to be ourselves.

Today I am grateful for my friends.

*The coming to consciousness is not a discovery of some
new thing; it is a long and painful return to that which
has always been.*

—Helen Luke

When a few guys in Ohio first developed the Twelve
Steps of Alcoholics Anonymous, they didn't just sit
down to devise a way to help alcoholics. The Steps were
born out of the pain and desperation of men in the
grips of a disease that seemed hopeless and terminal.
By trial and error they wrestled with this grip of addiction, slowly uncovering an approach that was helping
them to stay sober. It was only after awakening in their
new life of sobriety that they started to define and
write down the steps they had taken.

In some ways, to reach our awakening we all must
pass through the same process of pain and challenge
that those men in Ohio did. No life is free of pain. The
best of us take our pain and seek to use it as a learning
tool. We ask how we can make something positive out
of our distress. We take stock of where we are and accept it as our starting point for moving forward. When
we awaken to consciousness through the Twelve Steps,
it is a unique and personal story, and yet it is a universal human story.

Today I give thanks for my growing consciousness.

The problem is this: skills learned in danger require the presence of danger to be effective.

—Wayne Muller

Many of us had stressful childhoods. Some of us lived in chaotic households. Some of us were badly treated by the people we relied on to take care of us. Life often felt dangerous, but we developed skills to deal with the chaos. Some of us learned to keep all our thoughts and feelings to ourselves, some of us learned to please those around us, and some of us learned to avoid all confrontation or disagreement.

These childhood skills, learned through hard lessons in the presence of danger, may have become fixed in our immature minds as the best answers for a lifetime. But in our adult lives, those dangers may no longer be present. No one is beating us up anymore, but we are still flinching. The door is open for us to walk out, but we now must learn the skills of living in a safer world. We can take small steps by saying how we feel, by opening our hearts to trusted friends, and by asking for what we would like and being generous with others. These skills can be learned, just as our childhood skills were learned, and as we gain this knowledge, we have more and more rewarding lives.

Today I will take some risks that are my privilege as an adult, even if they seem risky.

Where there is fear, we lose the way of our spirit.

—Mahatma Gandhi

We don't like to admit that we are afraid. But when we won't admit the feeling, we can't deal with it. By denying our fears, we don't get stronger, we weaken ourselves. Denying fear doesn't get rid of problems, it only reinforces them. In the end, if we don't handle fear well, it rules us.

Fear is a universal human emotion, and we cannot eradicate it. We must learn how to handle the hot coals of fear. When we learn how, they don't have to be destructive. Handling fear begins with self-knowledge. We first learn that the unsettling feeling we have may be fear. Our desire to run away, or the tight knot in our gut, may be fear. That admission to ourselves can be followed by talking about it to a friend or a sponsor. Sometimes just speaking the fear out loud to someone we trust is enough to put it back in perspective. We have handled it.

Today I will notice my feelings and respond to feelings of fear in constructive ways.

Between stimulus and response, man has the freedom to choose.

—Stephen R. Covey

Ancient wise men first identified that crucial gap in time between the moment we first sense something and the response we give. They taught meditation principles focusing on this distinction and spent hours in contemplation that led to deep inner peace and serenity. Most of us, in our busy lives, do not devote hours and days to that focus, but we can learn to practice the crucial wisdom of chosen response instead of instant reflex.

Reactivity is like a knee-jerk response. It comes from a primitive part of our brains. If we haven't learned of that brief gap between the stimulus and our response, then we don't even know we have a choice. We might say, "I couldn't help it. If he hadn't done that, I wouldn't have done what I did." At that point we are still immature and weak. When we gain awareness of this tiny bit of time to choose the best response, we step from immaturity into the strength of a grown man.

Today I will become more aware of that moment of choice between a stimulus and my response.

How many cares one loses when one decides not to be something, but to be someone.

—Coco Chanel

Why are we working so hard? What are we striving toward? Do we want to achieve some important accomplishment, or do we want to be someone we respect? Naturally we don't have just one aim. We have many goals and hopes, but what are the most important ones?

When we focus on becoming the best kind of person we know how to be, we leave behind all our anxieties about how well we can perform. We still need to accomplish tasks and do our work, but the important thing now is the kind of person we are while we are doing them. Are we honest? Are we considerate of others? Is our heart open to the world? Do we take responsibility for our actions? When we fulfill the personal qualities that we admire, we can allow ourselves some slack for mistakes and imperfection in our achievements.

Today I am grateful that I am becoming someone I respect.

*God should be sought, but we cannot find God. We can
only be found by God.*

—Henri Nouwen

In our spiritual development, we get to know the mysteries and paradoxes in our own lives that great thinkers have written about. True spiritual development is an ever-deepening lesson in powerlessness and letting go. We seek God, but our seeking is really only our preparation to receive God. We don't make the willful decision to find God. We only decide to be open and to stop standing in the way of God's purposes in our lives.

When a man falls asleep, sleep doesn't come when he works at it. It comes only when, in his mind, he stops working at anything. He decides to go to bed and fall asleep but then he simply lies back and allows it to happen. If, in his mind, he is still busy working, he will not sleep. Something like that is true in all matters of letting go. We must learn how to stop getting in the way of spiritual influences in our lives, and our only power is to become entirely ready to receive them.

*Today I will let go of my self-centered willfulness and
be open to the greater powers at work.*

Spring is when you feel like whistling even with a shoe full of slush.

—Doug Larson

Life is never just one thing. It is quite possible to feel optimistic and happy even when some things are not right with us. An optimistic outlook gives us energy to handle the harder things that we have to deal with. Research shows that people who have a positive attitude have a stronger immune system, are healthier, live longer, and are even more likely to recover from serious illness.

To believe in hopeful outcomes is largely a matter of choice. Many of us have experienced big disappointments and defeats in life. But having come this far, we can look back and see that somehow we had the capacity to deal with it. The Second Step guides us to believe in hopeful possibilities. We can't say that things will always turn out just the way we hope, but that we can cope with whatever happens.

Today I choose to believe that a Power greater than myself can help me deal with life, and I have reason to be optimistic.

Anger is a great energizer if you don't get stuck in it.

—Lavonne Stewart

Many of us have to face up to our anger and the negative ways we have handled it. For most men, the real problem is not anger itself, but how we express it. Some of us never express it; others get abusive when we express it. Either way calls for more growth. Often, people confuse anger with abuse. They may say, "I just have to express my feelings, and when I'm angry, I have to let it out." Other people say, "Anger is so hurtful. I will avoid it at all costs."

Healing requires that we look to see the sources of our anger, how we have expressed it or failed to, and then learn how to say our feelings honestly and with respect. When we see what we are actually angry about, it gives us energy, it motivates us. It's a life force. There is no rule that we have to show our anger in destructive ways. We can be flat-out angry at someone we love and still maintain the respect we hold for that person. It is possible to learn to look at a friend and say, "I feel angry about this and I'm here to tell you about it because I care about our friendship."

Today I will accept my angry feelings as a source of life energy, and I will find honest, respectful ways to show it.

Discipline is remembering what you want.

—David Campbell

Not everyone chooses recovery easily. We were attached to our addictions and codependency, even if we didn't want their consequences. They were not only our masters; we were also loyal to them. They gave us comfort, pleasure, and a high that nothing else could match. So where did we find motivation to change?

Somewhere within our souls we longed for something of greater quality. We didn't want to sacrifice our future for the fleeting pleasures or false escapes. We saw that our actions were ruining our own lives and the lives of our loved ones. We always thought we would change someday, and even while our lives were careening out of control, we promised ourselves to change tomorrow or sometime in the future. It was our greater vision, our longing for a better life, that led us to try the Twelve Step recovery program. Out of wanting something better we found the motivation to enter recovery.

Today I know that deep in my soul lies a desire to be a good man.

Thought is action in rehearsal.

—Sigmund Freud

We sometimes indulge ourselves in fantasies and images of things we would like to do, or in euphoric recall of what we did in the past. Thoughts are powerful forces, and the ways we use them will shape our development. An Olympic diver creates vivid images of the perfect dive in his mind as part of his training because his thoughts help him perform at the crucial moment. Even in recovery, we are sometimes tempted to revisit former ecstatic moments from our using days, or to dream about a return to using but with better control the next time. We need to keep in mind that these thoughts serve as rehearsals for later action. They only weaken our recovery.

What kind of thoughts shall we cultivate in our minds? We can picture ourselves feeling relaxed and peaceful, having the craving lifted from us. We can picture ourselves maintaining a serene detachment while confronted with crisis. We can picture a situation with a loved one in which we say what we need to say and feel good about staying true to ourselves. This is the way to use our minds to rehearse for future action.

Today I will hold an image of myself feeling relaxed and safe, even in the midst of confusion around me.

When one door closes another door opens; but we often look so long and so regretfully upon the closed door that we do not see the ones which open for us.

—Alexander Graham Bell

Change is a basic fact of life and with every change comes a loss. Even winning the lottery entails the loss of our life before the big win. During some periods of our life, we feel we are stuck and nothing changes, or we feel trapped in a situation we would love to change. Other times a change occurs that we would never choose, and we have to find a way to continue living with the new reality.

Coping with the closing and opening of doors is a fundamental spiritual matter. We are pilgrims on a journey and much of what happens along our way is beyond our control. Today will bring some things that we did not expect and with the changes will be new possibilities that we did not expect. So we hold the spiritual attitude that while we cannot control what happens, we can choose how we will respond.

Today I pray for the spiritual vision to see the doors that open for me.

My dear child, you must believe in God in spite of what the clergy tell you.

—Benjamin Jowett

We come to the Twelve Step program of recovery from many different backgrounds. Some of us already have a very solid spiritual base to call upon. Some of us have a blank, undeveloped sense of spirituality and an open mind. Some of us had negative or even abusive experiences with organized religion, so we turned away from all ideas of spirituality. Now we are following a path that asks us to turn our lives and will over to God, and our past experience may tell us to say no to such a proposition.

Still, we want to recover, and our previous methods didn't work, so now we are willing to have an open mind about "the God thing." Maybe we can learn something we never understood before. The concept of God was controversial even among the men who first developed this path. They all knew that spiritual reliance was crucial to recovery, but they didn't all believe in God in the same way. So they landed on the phrase, "God as we understood Him." Wisely, they made the program's spirituality a very big tent, and there is room for every individual's beliefs.

Today I am grateful for the spirituality that this program has nurtured within me.

Love at first sight is easy to understand. It's when two people have been looking at each other for years that it becomes a miracle.

—Sam Levenson

True intimacy introduces us to ourselves. A loving relationship is the greatest therapy. When we first fall in love, we are filled with optimism and the greatest hopes for fulfillment of our dreams. We cling to all the best qualities of the person we fall in love with and we look past those things we don't like. But living in an intimate partnership takes us beyond the edge of what we have learned. It is truly an adult developmental challenge.

Most of us fall in love and soon find ourselves in over our heads. We haven't had experience as adults in sustaining the openness and vulnerability we have walked into. We may gradually begin to feel too vulnerable and exposed. The relationship tests our ability to trust someone who has this much access to our inner self. We are tempted to become cranky, edgy, or overly sensitive. We may test our partner's love by asking, if you love me, will you do such and such? We begin to try to control our partner so we don't feel so vulnerable. All these temptations are holdover behaviors from our less mature selves. So we must reach for our more mature selves, breathe deeply, and trust that we can survive while being so close and vulnerable.

Today I will turn to my Higher Power for guidance in going forward in trust while being vulnerable.

I go to nature to be soothed and healed, and to have my senses put in order.

—John Burroughs

In the Twelve Steps we see the term *God* several times. But from the program's beginning, there have been atheists and agnostics using and valuing the Steps as their guide for life. Many men do not relate to a personal God. They do, however, experience the meaning and spirit of their group and the restoring powers of nature. That is why the founders of Alcoholics Anonymous included the phrase "God as we understood Him."

Whether a personal God is real to us or not, nature is there for us as a healing and refreshing source. We don't have to go on a major trip to the mountains or fishing in the wilderness to find this source. We find it in the sky, the clouds, and the magical moon; we find it in the intricate structure of a leaf, a massive tree in the park, or a wild bird visiting a feeder. There is no more clear evidence of the generous gifts that come unbidden than in nature. And we can rest in the Power greater than ourselves shown in creation and the forces of nature.

Today I will be soothed and healed by nature all around.

We must find some spiritual basis for living, else we die.
—Bill Wilson

When one of the founders of Alcoholics Anonymous wrote these words, he was speaking from the perspective of a recovering man. He knew that his addiction would kill him if he didn't base his life on a spiritual footing. There is also such a thing as being spiritually dead while our physical bodies are still alive. Whether we are recovering from addiction or codependency, or walking some other healing path, our life force is rooted in our spiritual connection.

Just as an addiction grows and progresses through the span of our lives, so too, if we are consciously attentive, our spiritual development continues through the years of our lives. We grow stronger, become more accepting of ourselves and others, and feel more connected to the people and the world we live in.

Today conscious contact with my creator keeps me alive.

*You see the one that I am, not the one that I was. But
the one that I was is also still part of myself.*

—Jean Amery

Our stories are central to our recovery. We tell them
because they remind us where we came from. We live
in the present moment, but our history is part of our
identity. It isn't the total of our identity, but it in-
forms our healing. It's the mine where we dig for the
nuggets of wisdom for living today, and it gives us the
drive and encouragement to continue our progress.
We don't tell our stories to wallow in the shame and
guilt we felt or to gain sympathy for our suffering.
And we don't tell them to revel in the euphoria of the
highs we experienced.

In telling our stories, others get to know us better
because our history is part of our very selves. In that
process, we cannot help but listen to ourselves speak
the truth, and thereby we put together the puzzle pieces
of our selves. Taking the risk of saying where we came
from provides the rewards of feeling accepted by others.

*I am grateful for telling my story and knowing that I
am more than the man I once was.*

Listen to your body. Do not be a blind and deaf tenant.
—Dr. George Sheehan

We were taught that masculinity means ignoring pain, disregarding the sensations that arise within our bodies. A warrior in battle needs to do that in order to save his life. When a man can ignore his pain because of a more pressing goal, he has a valuable skill. But we aren't living in a battle zone every day. And a wise man uses his skills selectively. When we are driving down an open highway on a sunny, warm day, we use different skills than when driving on ice.

Part of our recovery requires that we grow beyond some of the stereotypes of what a man is. A one-trick pony can't adapt to a new show. When we are in the safety of an intimate relationship, we need to know what we feel and express it. We need the skills to pay attention to our internal messages, because they are also guides.

Today I will have the wisdom to listen to the messages of my body and my heart.

Although the world is full of suffering, it is also full of overcoming it.

—Helen Keller

We are born into a life with both pain and joy. That mix is inevitable, no matter what our status in life. If today's combination seems more filled with difficulty or challenge, it also contains the possibilities for coping with it. We can take some steps today that will move us toward overcoming our challenges. We must avoid feeling defeated if we cannot totally fix our problems all at once. And most certainly, there are unseen forces at work, forces that continually bring change.

Let us accept that life always changes. Never can we place a clamp on some perfect day and hold ourselves there permanently. So we ride the ups and downs, we meet our pain and suffering, and we overcome it.

Today, as I face difficulty and rise to its challenges, I will have an attitude of acceptance.

Dream as if you'll live forever. Live as if you'll die tomorrow.

—James Dean

To live as if we will die tomorrow means to feel very alive right now. It means to be spiritually alert in the present moment with an open heart and full awareness of our experience. To dream as if we will live forever means we hold a vision and a sense of values that act as a compass on our path, directing our daily choices.

We know how it felt to be lost or trapped and already half dead. That was before our rebirth in recovery. One of life's paradoxes is that when we accept our ultimate powerlessness of death, we are freed to live life at its fullest. This is not the path that most adults follow. It is easy to lapse into a less alive, less spiritually alert style. But on our healing journey, we cannot afford that.

Today I am grateful for this day and this moment of life.

I don't want everyone to like me; I should think less of myself if some people did.

—Henry James

When we don't know ourselves very well, we may be desperate to have everyone like us. Sometimes we even notice more intently that one person who doesn't seem to like us than the many who do. We are looking outward to verify that we are okay. Of course it feels good to have someone else like and respect us. Until we begin to know and accept ourselves, we have an unquenchable, unselective thirst for more applause from others. In that condition, the search for others' approval drives us like the need for survival.

It is amazing how our sense of ourselves grows as we live in the Twelve Step program. We get to know ourselves by working the Steps, and we develop into the kind of men we respect. Now, having others like us is no longer a survival need. It is a wonderful benefit of being part of the human community.

Today I am grateful for the true friendships that I have in my life.

If you are walking through hell, keep going.

                        —Winston Churchill

Some days, some weeks, even some years seem like hell.
We give our best to life and still it continues to be hard.
A future with some measure of pain and problems is
inevitable from the very day of our birth. That may
seem like a bleak reality, and it is what we may call hell.
But it is also the very thing that shapes our learning
and development into good men.

These times of challenge and heartache call us to
keep going. They are a source of spiritual lessons for
us. If today finds us in the midst of such difficulty, we
can know that we are never alone. Our Higher Power is
always with us. We can talk to a friend and let him
know what is happening in our life. And we can also
know that, as bad as any time might be, life is always a
mixture that includes some blessings and something
to be grateful for.

Today I will keep going forward.

An expert is a man who has made all the mistakes that can be made in a narrow field.

—Niels Bohr

At the time they happen, mistakes are always deeply regrettable. No one ever sets out to make a mistake. Fortunately we are not seeking perfection. We weren't born fully clothed with an instruction book on how to live. We don't learn anything new from doing the things we already have down pat. Mistakes are how we learn, and some of those lessons are painful indeed. A man who is afraid to risk a mistake shields himself from growing.

So we take risks, knowing we will make mistakes. There is no shame in a mistake that we learn from. It is said that the truly wise man keeps his beginner's attitude and is always open to learning. Many of us can say that if mistakes create an expert, then we must be well qualified already. And, in fact, for those of us who have learned from them, we truly are smarter and stronger for the experience. The key is first to discard the notion of perfectionism, then to take the reasonable risks that may lead to mistakes, and finally to learn the lessons contained in them.

Today I am grateful for my life experience, and I will continue to take reasonable risks and grow.

May

□ □ □ □ □ □ □

Our Lord has written the promise of resurrection, not in books alone but in every leaf of springtime.

—Martin Luther

Springtime is a perfect metaphor for renewed life, recovery, and resurrection. All around us we see the buds of leaves and flowers bursting forth in celebration. Just like nature, we, too, experience our personal springtime of renewal. Our personal anniversaries are worthy of celebration, whether it be one day, one month, or many years of recovery.

Some people are shy about celebrating their days and years of recovery. Maybe they feel unworthy, or they don't want to draw attention to themselves. But the true spirit of celebration is humility. It's not because we have worked so hard that we deserve it; it's that we have been given the gift promised in the Twelve Steps. Because we submit to the grace of God, we celebrate the gift we have received.

Today I see the symbols of renewed life within me and all around.

If you come to a fork in the road, take it.

—Yogi Berra

The humor in this quotation points to some deeper wisdom. The fact is, we all come to forks in the road of life, and we have to choose which way to go. Sometimes we cannot see a clear best choice. Sometimes we know what the best choice would be, but we cannot face the losses or the pain it would entail. Many of us have stopped at the fork in the road and just sat there for a long, long time, refusing to take either way.

The healthy, creative, constructive life requires some risk taking. Even when we are not sure which is the best way to go, it may be better to try one of them than to just stay stuck. Certainly it is wise to stop, consider our choices, and not be too hasty or impulsive. But after we think and weigh the options, making a choice will lead to new information, which will then influence our next choices. That is how we follow a creative and lively path for ourselves.

Today I will remember that some risk taking is healthy.

When you have got an elephant by the hind leg, and he
is trying to run away, it's best to let him run.

—Abraham Lincoln

We know what it feels like to have an elephant by the
hind leg when he wants to run. We have held on to our
addictive and codependent ways, thinking we were in
control and refusing to face the reality that we were
about to get trampled. Now we can be grateful for the
guidance of Step One. When we could admit we were
not in control, that changed everything.

Some of us knew we were out of control but didn't
know where to go from there. We were living in
despair, but with no place to turn. Steps One and Two
pointed the way to a spiritual release. We were told
that if we "let the elephant go," we could get help from
a Higher Power. This new way of thinking gave us a
whole different take on our life. We can let go and we
will survive.

Today I am grateful for the life-changing option of
letting go.

Working so hard for the rewards we want, we miss the gifts, already present, that God wants to give us.

—Anonymous

We cannot win many of the good things in life; we can only receive them. It is like falling asleep. No one can will himself to sleep. If we could, there would be no such thing as a sleepless night. The harder we try, the more awake we become. We can only *allow* ourselves to fall asleep. We cannot create a sunny day or a beautiful sight in nature, but we can block them from our awareness. We cannot fall in love by force of will, but we can prevent it from happening by our willfulness or busy habits. Our raging appetites and anxious state of mind can drive us willy-nilly in search of satisfaction—while more profound gifts are already in our hands.

Many valuable gifts are available only if we stay open to receive them. A wise man grows past our society's mainstream idea that anything worth having requires hard work. The ultimate truth is that God's grace provides what we need. Our work is in learning how to let go and be receptive.

Today I will open myself to the gifts already in my hands.

Don't brood on what's past, but never forget it either.
— Thomas H. Raddall

When we make big changes in our lives for the better, as we have all done, we naturally grieve the time we lost by not learning our lessons sooner. There's no way to avoid that grief, but there's no point in dwelling on it. Some of us get hooked by feelings of regret. We brood over the ways we let others down, and we wish we could relive certain events and do better with them this time. It is important for us all to release the past—let it go.

Our life is now. If we spend our conscious moments living in the past and regretting our mistakes, we never get on with living a good life in the present. A truly humble man accepts the forgiveness of others and the forgiveness of his Higher Power. He accepts the universal truth that we are all broken in some ways, and our self-acceptance isn't based upon what we did or didn't do in the past, but on how we live today.

Today I look back at where I have come from and feel grateful for a new life.

Memory is the diary we all carry about with us.

—Oscar Wilde

Our memories create the substance of our identity. People who lose their memory lose any sense of who they are. Some of us have memories of painful events in our childhood, or of traumas that changed our image of ourselves. Those of us who were abused by parents have to learn in adulthood to fill those gaps by becoming good parents to ourselves. Some of us have become trapped at a younger stage of development by painful memories. Now, it is essential to our healing that we not perpetuate our own abuse.

We have to learn to include ourselves in the human family. No matter what we experienced, no matter what we feel, it is all part of what it means to be human. We can heal our memories, not by changing them, but by making peace with them so we are free to live in the present. A man can imagine the little boy he once was— and imagine taking that youngster on his lap and promising him that he will take care of him and keep him safe.

Today I will be a good parent to myself and treat myself with love and respect.

Everything becomes a little different as soon as it is spoken out loud.

—Hermann Hesse

Central to our healing and recovery is telling our story and hearing the stories others have to tell. Something changes when we first speak out loud to another person to tell what we were like, what we have experienced, and what we feel now. Most people feel great relief when they say what they have on their minds. Often we don't fully know what we feel or think until we put it into words. The telling of it to an attentive listener bridges the gap between us.

Putting our stories into words gives them a form they didn't have before and gives us handles to begin to deal with our experience. When we tell the story of our pain, our mistakes, and our triumphs, the words are the symbols that allow us to let go and move on.

Today I will talk to someone about my experience, describing either a small feeling or a big one.

Some things have to be believed to be seen.

—Ralph Hodgson

Under the guidance of this recovery program we "came to believe that a Power greater than ourselves could restore us to sanity." Coming to believe something is a process. It might begin by borrowing someone else's faith, trying it on as we might try on a shirt. We don't start with a firm conviction. We don't grow instantly from no faith to absolute faith. It might begin by seeing that forces are at work beyond our control, easing our terrible cravings or supporting us through the worst times.

Sometimes faith develops very slowly, like the first sprout of an acorn in the spring. At our meetings we encounter men who are like mighty oaks, but years ago, they were just beginning to send up tender sprouts. This process certainly takes us beyond what we can explain with rational description. We don't have to understand it.

Today I am grateful for the faith that allows me to see what I could not otherwise see.

God as the ultimate mystery of being is beyond thinking.

—Joseph Campbell

The child's profound question "Where did I come from?" never really gets answered as long as we live. We learn to settle for things that point to an answer, for bits of evidence of partial answers. Holy scriptures tell us what inspired and wise people said over the millennia. But in the end, our thinking isn't big enough to encompass or understand the ultimate mystery.

Yet it seems to be in the nature of our human race to think in spiritual terms and to embrace mystery. We are in awe when we see the vastness of the ocean, when we gaze across the vista from a mountainside, or when we look through a microscope at the inner workings of a cell. This feeling of awe and beauty, and the mystery it evokes, is the spiritual impulse. The mystery brought us here, and when we follow it, we can learn to trust it. It gives us our birthright to be here and it will care for us.

Today I am in the care of God, and I will accept the comfort of trusting God.

*One of the oldest human needs is having someone
wonder where you are when you don't come home
at night.*

—Margaret Mead

Many of us grew up with a loving mother who gave us life and cared for our needs. Others among us had mothers who were missing from our lives, either physically or emotionally. Perhaps no word in any language carries more weight or more feelings than the word *mother*. It carries images of comfort, undying love, first intimacy, and complete acceptance. Few mothers ever totally fulfill those images.

As we become adults, we have a more realistic understanding of our relationship with our mother. She was a real human being, not a stereotype, and not perfect. We longed for her approval and her love, as all children do. We had angry feelings toward her sometimes, and guilt about the ways we hurt her. It is our adult task to make peace with her, living or dead, to forgive her for what we did not get and for how we were hurt, and to accept forgiveness for our mistakes. Only after we have made that peace are we truly emancipated adults and free to love others fully.

Today I seek peace with my mother.

*It is only by risking ourselves from one hour to another
that we live at all.*

—William James

We all know men who seem to be empty bodies, walking through life. These are the guys who never talk about anything personal and never let anyone get to know them. Many of them love to complain about their job, their wife or girlfriend, their boss, the government, or anything outside themselves. These guys will talk about sports or the weather but never about real events or personal experiences. Many of us have been these men.

When we wake up to a real life, we become present; we are alive to our experiences, our sensations, and our feelings. This requires that we drop the shield of deadness and become personal. It involves risk and makes life incredibly interesting.

*Today I will take the risk to be present to my life in
every minute, every hour.*

Just as we took refuge in being special, we can learn to take refuge in being ordinary, not being in charge, not being the center of the universe.

—Wayne Muller

In our addictive and codependent minds, we were prone to feeling special. We felt grandiose about our power to fix others, or about our power to walk on the edge of danger and not get hurt. We thought we could handle things that most people couldn't. Some of us felt especially bad and shameful, more shameful than everyone else. We thought recovery was fine for others but it wasn't what we needed, or it wasn't going to work for us.

True self-esteem is not based on feeling special or better than others. A large ingredient of true self-esteem is self-respecting humility. We are all much more alike than we are different, and we are connected to each other on the basic levels of life and death, pain and joy, and the need to give and receive love. When we make friends with other men and really let them know us, we feel our common humanity and a strong sense of self-acceptance and self-esteem.

Today I will notice my connection with all others, the people I like and the ones I dislike, the people I know and the people who are strangers.

*You can't control the wind, but you can adjust
your sails.*

—Fortune cookie message

Sailing is both peaceful and adventurous. Imagine being on a sailboat, working the sails to use the wind for quiet, controlled movement or for exciting speed as you skim across the water. It's a skill that improves with experience. You learn to work with the wind and apply it to your advantage. Anyone who tries to sail his boat willfully, contrary to the conditions of the wind, gets nowhere.

A well-lived life also draws on experience, and we continue to learn as long as we live. Our male models told us that masculinity meant conquering our surroundings, and many of us instinctively saw competition and confrontation as a matter of personal honor. We believed that, as men, our self-esteem was tied to subduing any obstacle before us. But those were a boy's ideas about what a man is like.

As we grow wiser and genuinely stronger, we set our sails to work with the wind. We can neither stop the wind nor make it blow.

*Today I will watch the winds in my life and work with
them to live better.*

*It's not so much that we're afraid of change or so in
love with the old ways, but it's that place in between
that we fear ... It's Linus when his blanket is in the
dryer. There's nothing to hold on to.*

—Marilyn Ferguson

The big change for us is moving beyond our addiction
and codependency. Many of us didn't feel very attached to our addiction, but we didn't know what to
do without it. We didn't feel "normal" when we weren't
using, and it didn't seem right to stop taking charge of
others' problems. It was hard to imagine what else to
do with our time, and hard to build another way of
living.

In many other smaller ways, we are called on to let
go of what is familiar and move into what is not yet
known. This is an uncomfortable but very creative
space. We know our growth was stopped by our old
ways. Now, with the courage to tolerate the discomfort, we can leave our less mature selves behind and
grow to become better men.

*Today I will tolerate feeling awkward and
uncomfortable while I keep growing.*

There is no smaller package in the world than that of a person all wrapped up in himself.

—William Sloane Coffin

In self-centeredness, we are trapped within the confines of our own skin. It is a self-indulgence that stifles and chokes our emotional development by continuously turning us back into our own limitations, pain, and fears. The grandiose feeling of superiority is not the only way that self-centeredness grabs and holds us; feelings of shame and self-pity can also trap us. To liberate ourselves from these traps, we first get acquainted with them and name the feelings, which gives us some power over them. Next, we get outside ourselves by reaching out to help someone else who is genuinely in need.

When we have a cause or a purpose greater than our own selfish goals, we escape the boundaries of our self. That's the spiritual move toward participating in the larger whole.

Today I will help someone simply out of generosity, or I will help with a cause that's greater than myself.

*Gossip needn't be false to be evil—there's a lot of truth
that shouldn't be passed around.*

—Frank A. Clark

To be a friend is a trust placed in us. Naturally, as we
get to know someone better, and we grow closer over
time, he lets us into his more private and personal
world, and he does that in a spirit of trust. In a sense
he is saying we may come past the fence that keeps
most people out because he trusts us. Maybe he even
lets us know some guarded secrets about his life. We
need to be sure that we live up to the trust placed in us.
Our self-respect and our character are at stake: how
loyally do we honor that trust?

When we attend our meetings, we hear many things
that are spoken in trust. Hearing someone's story is a
privilege and an honor and with that comes our duty
to honor and protect the privacy of our fellow members. When someone takes us into his privacy, it becomes our job to protect it. If we fail to keep his trust,
it reflects on us as not worthy of the honor.

*Today I am grateful for the chance to know other men
and women so well that they share their private lives
with me. I honor that trust by protecting their privacy.*

*A dwarf standing on the shoulders of a giant may see
farther than a giant himself.*

—Robert Burton

We all stand on the shoulders of those who have been
our teachers, and on the shoulders of those who taught
our teachers. When we pick a sponsor for our recovery,
we look for someone we admire and trust, someone
who has demonstrated success in his recovery.

Perhaps we feel we have a long way to go and a lot to
learn. Perhaps we are struck by the big job we have
ahead. But all we need to do is make progress. And we
don't have to reinvent the wheel. When we learn from
our sponsor and from other people in our recovery
community who are making progress, we get to stand
on their shoulders. They let us see much more than we
could see alone.

*Today I am grateful for all the benefits of having a good
sponsor.*

When you aim for perfection you discover it's a moving target.

—George Fisher

In our desire for control, we seek the ultimate control of perfection. We try to relieve our anxieties and self-doubts by achieving it, but in fact we perpetuate our unease by seeking what cannot be attained. Some of us say, "I'm not a perfectionist because I am far from perfect," only proving that we are always measuring ourselves with that yardstick.

The way to resolve this dilemma is to get a different yardstick. Instead of measuring how far we are from perfect, we could measure whether we are learning anything new. Or we can ask ourselves if we have continued to get back on the path when we veer off course. Knowing we will make mistakes, we can ask ourselves if we take responsibility for them. Knowing some things will go wrong, no matter how well we plan, we can include in our plans a vision to accept mistakes as part of the package.

Today I will try to learn from whatever happens, and when something goes wrong, I will accept it and deal with it.

How we spend our days is, of course, how we spend our lives.

—Annie Dillard

Today *is* our life. Even though we are drawn to live in the past or have fears and hopes for the future, we only exist in the present. This moment is all we have, and it is enough. There is no need to center our thoughts on how things will turn out in the future because we are alive right now, and this is our life. Our memories exist only in our minds; they enrich the present, but we have no opportunity to relive them.

As we live in this moment and center our awareness in this moment, we have a sense that we can deal with it. Feeling overwhelmed comes from trying to take too big of a bite of time. It's more than anyone can swallow. In this moment, as we sit in our place, we have sensations of sight and sound and touch. We can deal with this moment and that is all we need to do . . . ever. Centered in this very time and this very place, we regain our peace of mind and our ability to live well.

Today is all I need, for today is my life.

When you lose, do not lose the lesson.

—H. Jackson Brown, Jr.

The only mistakes we are doomed to repeat are the ones we fail to learn from. Life is a matter of approximating our goals, seldom a matter of hitting the bullseye. We take risks, sometimes we fail to understand what we are dealing with, and sometimes we just indulge ourselves in what we want regardless of what is good for us. So, in some ways, we are constantly remeasuring the difference between what we aimed for and what we actually achieved.

If we only mourn the loss or berate ourselves for missing the target and never use it to learn, we have truly lost something important. It is when we call on our inner resources and learn the lesson that we get better and stronger. Learning is the most important part of our life journey.

Today I will look for the lessons in my mistakes and let go of defeatist attitudes.

*A man does not seek to see himself in running water,
but in still water. For only what is itself still can impart
stillness to others.*

—Chuang-tse

Our own reactivity has often escalated a problem
rather than helped to resolve it. But we can learn to be
less reactive. All of us have a range of responses. At our
worst we may lash out in abusive anger. At our best we
try to be tolerant and understanding. When we are ex-
hausted or depleted in other ways, we are more prone
to react from our worst self. And our harsh reaction
only makes a crisis worse.

We can change our pattern of reactivity and give our
best response by developing an inner calm. Then we always have access to our better self, and we are less
prone to take things personally. That doesn't mean we
are always placid or passive, because sometimes our
best self needs to rise up and say *no!* When we are calm,
we can respond most effectively, either with open tolerance or with a "no" if it is called for.

*Today I will maintain an inner calm as I deal with the
issues that arise.*

Whoever thinks that marriage is a fifty-fifty proposition doesn't know the half of it.

—Franklin P. Jones

Naturally we expect our intimate partnerships to be built on equality and mutuality. Sometimes we get so focused on the role our partner is playing that we lose focus on our own. A good intimate partnership works when we stay focused on being a worthy partner and stop keeping score.

We nourish our intimate relationship by being respectful, kind, and generous, whether or not we feel our partner is doing the same. That doesn't mean that we never talk about what we want or hope for from our partner. It simply means that our loving attitude isn't contingent on whether we get what we want. We know what a good partner is like, and when we provide that, it enhances the whole relationship and inspires our partner to respect us and respond in kind.

Today I will be the best partner I know how to be, regardless of what I receive.

Seeing first one's own defects and shortcomings is Humility; the fruit of vision is tolerance.

—Ernest Kurtz and Katherine Ketcham

The word *humble* has its roots in the Latin word for earth, *humus*. That doesn't mean that if I am humble I feel like dirt. It means that the earth is truly my mother. My flesh and bones, like all living creatures, are made of earth—nothing more and nothing less.

When I gain humility, I have myself in perspective. I like myself and I see how much I have in common with all my fellow human beings. This is truly a gift that I receive as part of living a spiritual life. It means I have acceptance and peace of mind. I don't have to constantly compete. I can make mistakes and still have the possibility of repairing them. I can be okay even when no one is paying attention to me.

Today I will be open to receiving the gift of humility.

> *Old man whose sperm swims in my veins come back in*
> *love, come back in pain.*

—Toi Derricotte

A man who never knew his father said, "My father had no influence on me." Then, as he pondered that thought further, he realized his father had had a great influence on him by his absence. In fact, he had searched all his life to learn what his father was like and had often wondered if his father would be proud of him.

Many of us grew up feeling the absence of our fathers, either because they were physically gone or because they were emotionally disconnected from us. We patched together a youth in which we grew up and became adult men, but we continue to wonder about that man whose genes shape us. What was he like?

For some of us it is still possible, as grown men, to change our relationships with our fathers, to bring up personal topics with them, to ask about their lives. For many of us that isn't possible, but all of us can learn to live in better ways. We can now develop genuine personal relationships with other men who have real feelings. And we become happier, more courageous, and wholesome men by doing so.

Today I will have a genuine personal conversation with
another man.

*When I was small I was very naughty and my father
chased me with his belt to give me a thrashing. Maybe
that was how I got accustomed to running.*

—Fermin Cacho, 1992 Olympic champion

Not all bad things are all bad. All of us can look back at
things that happened to us, bad experiences, painful
times, and still say that we became better men for the
experience. Men who have had cancer, men who spent
years in prison, even unjustly accused, men who were
abused—all have said that they used the experience to
grow and improve. That is the sign of a good man.

Artists say that great design often occurs when they
are forced to work within the limits of a situation. The
outcome is not their original vision but an evolution
into something surprising and wonderful. In this program we hear the stories of many others who struggled
with great challenges but used their struggles toward
constructive results. A great runner doesn't become
great because he was chased by his father with a belt,
but because he used his experiences to make something positive out of it. Our recovery is an example of
that very thing.

*Today I will seek ways to turn my challenges into
creative responses.*

Those who contemplate the beauty of the earth find reserves of strength that will endure as long as life lasts.

—Rachel Carson

Where do we turn for contemplation and contact with a spiritual source? Many men find it in nature. They look out the window at a handsome tree. They go for a walk outdoors, feed the birds, let themselves be awed by the sight of the moon on a dark night. The natural world offers our most direct, tangible contact with something eternal. We are part of something much larger than ourselves, something that endures for the ages.

The beauty of nature inspires awe, which is a form of reverence. We walk along a canyon rim and God is there. We walk through prairie grasses and wildflowers teeming with wildlife, the wind blows in our faces, and our spirits rise. These natural beauties endure forever.

Today, as I look at the natural world, I see God.

An error doesn't become a mistake until you refuse to correct it.

—Orlando A. Battista

In our lives, we have always been drawn to extremes. If it isn't white, it must be black. If a little bit feels good, we take a lot. If we are going to do something, only perfection is good enough. So if we don't win, we lose, and if we can't do it perfectly, we feel like a failure.

In this program we learn to seek progress, not perfection. And we can only make progress by trial and error. We learn nothing if we don't try new things and then learn from our errors. We don't jump into perfect sobriety the moment we decide to enter this program of recovery. When we surrender to our powerlessness over our addictions and codependency, we have to begin to learn how to live in a new way. It doesn't just happen all at once. So when we take our errors and our slips and agree to learn from them, we become stronger in our sobriety.

Today I accept my imperfection as a permanent condition, and I will keep coming back to the program of recovery.

*The first peace, which is the most important, is that
which comes within the souls of people when they realize
their relationship, their oneness, with the universe and
all its powers, and when they realize that at the center
of the universe dwells Wakan-Tanka, and that this
center is really everywhere, it is within each of us.*

—Black Elk

When we understand power and powerlessness, we
begin to find inner peace. We have often felt alone, isolated from others and from the world. Now we are
learning about relationships and our connection to all
things. Our biggest mistake was a childish notion that
power and control are up to the individual. We didn't
trust or even know about relationships and the forces
of the universe.

We are actually part of an awesome universe and we
have a place in it. When we develop our relationships
and understand our oneness with all others and the
forces at work, we understand that we are never alone.
We only participate in this big picture.

*Today I live as a relative to all people and the whole
world.*

*The kid doesn't chew tobacco, smoke, drink, curse, or
chase broads. I don't see how he can ever make it.*

—Richie Ashburn, Hall of Fame center fielder

We grew up with many misguided messages about
what it takes to be a real man. These ideas were fun in
some ways but led us down paths of self-defeating behavior. They gave us boyish ideas without pointing the
way to genuinely strong and masculine lives. Now we
know that a strong man has fun but still holds values
such as honesty, kindness, and generosity.

Toughness is a virtue in many situations, but no
one is more masculine than the guy with strength of
character. A truly strong man lends a hand to others;
he reflects daily on his own character and holds himself responsible. And he can be as sensual and playful
as the best of them.

*Today I am grateful to be walking on the path of a true
masculine life.*

Never let the fear of striking out get in your way.

—Babe Ruth

Fear is a normal emotion that many of us have to face. Some call it one of their character defects. We may have been more ruled by it than we admitted to ourselves. We allowed fear to be our guide when higher purposes told us we should make other choices. Because we honored our fears, we took refuge in controlling others, or in the fleeting ecstasies of our addictions. But that trap doesn't have to keep its grip on us. The best cure for fear is to confront it again and again. Fear of heights goes away when we repeatedly face high places.

Fear is just another emotion; it doesn't have to rule our choices. The best way to handle fear is to acknowledge the feeling and then put it in our back pocket while we move forward and do what we need to do. We also have the reassurance that we need not face anything alone. Our Higher Power is always with us. We focus on doing our best and turn the outcome over to the care of God as we understand God.

Today I will acknowledge my fears, pay attention to them, and then follow the guidance of my higher purposes.

*I have one request: may I never use my reason
against truth.*

—Elie Wiesel

Honesty with ourselves is a great asset in every situation we confront. The skill to look reality square in the face and call it what it is takes us a good distance toward coping with it. However, many of us also have the skill to spin or rationalize our actions so that we don't have to face something unpleasant. That skill provides us with excuses and evasions but it is the greatest betrayal of our selves. When we use our brain to cleverly cover the truth of our actions, we often believe our own lies, and then we're incapable of rectifying them.

Just as dishonesty builds and grows on itself, so does honesty. We cannot one day decide to be honest and change in a flash because we don't see all of our self-deceit yet. But we can make the decision to be as honest as we know how. Then we will soon be surprised by how much is revealed to us as the fog of our self-deceit lifts and our honesty builds upon itself.

*Today I will strive to see reality as it is and not shape it
to suit my ego's desires.*

June

□ □ □ □ □ □ □

No matter what accomplishments you achieve,
somebody helps you.

—Althea Gibson

Some of us can get so full of ourselves when we win a
race or get a raise that we think we did it all by ourselves. But the question is, what is really so good about
the idea of doing it all by ourselves? Isn't it just as good
to achieve something great and give credit to all those
who helped us? We live in a community of friends and
neighbors; we are all part of a larger system that holds
us up. We have teachers and mentors who help us on
our way. We have doctors who help us keep our bodies
healthy. We have loved ones who support us and give
us more meaning in our lives.

During our active addiction, some of us were so in-
vested in the idea of fierce individualism that we de-
valued anything that required help from others. That
was a limited and immature way of seeing things. The
paradox is that not until we could accept help could we
gain the strength required for a better life.

Today I feel very proud of my accomplishments and
very grateful for all the help I had in achieving them.

Always *and* never *are two words you should always
remember never to use.*

—Wendell Johnson

Words are powerful. We have a way of thinking in
terms of all or nothing, black or white, and seldom in
shades of gray. If we like something, we want more and
more of it. If we take on a project, we throw ourselves
into it with all we've got. But the truth is, life is mostly
somewhere between extremes. If a little of something is
good, more is not necessarily better. When we have a
bad day, it doesn't mean that our whole life is a mess.

If we say, "You always . . ." or "You never . . ." to a
friend or loved one, the discussion is sure to intensify.
If we use those words in conflict, the other person is
sure to feel misunderstood. *Always* and *never* are extreme words that are rarely accurate. We are learning to
live life in moderation and to think and see life more
honestly.

*Today I will remember to see the shades of gray, rather
than the extremes of black and white.*

Man's heart away from nature becomes hard.

—Standing Bear

The wisdom of Native American spirituality is deeply centered on the natural world. It teaches us to respect the earth and all natural things. It teaches us, as many world religions do, that we are made of earth and live by the gifts of nature. The word *humility* comes from the word *humus,* meaning "of the earth." When we become alienated or too far removed from nature, we become disconnected from ourselves. We lose our place and become willful.

Humility is not the same as shame. Humility is self-respecting and it expresses that we have a place in the entire web of life. One aspect of a spiritual life is the feeling of awe. Where better to return to the feeling of awe than in sight of a massive mountain, the sea, a powerful storm, or the intricate details of a flower or a stone.

Today I will return to the natural world around me, and with awe, I will give thanks.

When it comes to staying young, a mind lift beats a
face-lift any day.

—Marty Bucella

We can choose to focus our attention on the image we
present to others, or to focus on who we are on the inside. When we feel inadequate or empty, it may never
occur to us to do something about how we feel about
ourselves. Instead, we may have learned to try to control how others see us—as if that were the path to self-
esteem. In our recovery, we learn that the basis of true
self-esteem is to have values and follow them. No matter how successful a man becomes economically, no
matter how many achievements he can point to in the
world, it is never enough until he feels right about
himself as a person.

We can be grateful for a program that points the
way toward genuine success: true self-respect and
self-acceptance. That doesn't mean we never regret
something we have done; it means we make distinctions between who we are and what we have done.
When we have values and follow them, sometimes we
fall short of our own standards. Then we admit our
shortcomings and repair them. In so doing, our inner
self-acceptance is maintained and we once again affirm
who we are.

Today I am more concerned about the man I am than
about the image I show to others.

Wisdom doesn't necessarily come with age. Sometimes age just shows up all by itself.

—Tom Wilson

If we live long enough, we will grow old. During that time we will make plenty of mistakes and have plenty of opportunities to learn from them. However, sometimes we refuse to accept the lessons that are wrapped in our experience. We may be so determined to have what we want that we deny the truth of what we can actually have. We may be so prideful or so stubborn or so insecure that we defy the lessons we are being taught and refuse to open ourselves to a new idea. We grow older, but not smarter.

Some men become very grown-up and very strong in wisdom at a young age. They are blessed with an open, engaging attitude and a willingness to surrender to truth when it faces them. We should cultivate an attitude of learning, of openness to new lessons, and of willingness to learn the lessons taught by our mistakes.

Today I will learn from my experience and become a little stronger and a little wiser.

*Defeat may serve as well as victory to shake the soul
and let the glory out.*

—Edwin Markham

No one goes in search of a defeat so that he can have a
stirring spiritual experience. The real defeats are the
ones that we would never choose. They break our treas-
ures and shake our foundations. In the breaking, a defeat gives us a changed life to deal with. It forces us to
see things from an angle we never saw before. We start
from the empty feeling and the question: now what?

Defeat is inevitable in life. We aren't really adults
until we have confronted situations that we desperately wanted to conquer but could not. It is in learning
to accept the reality of powerlessness that we have the
first opportunity to become full adults. When a man
stops at defeat and feels only defeated, without finding
the wisdom to grow beyond it, he stays stuck in that
spot. In recovery and healing, we are learning that the
renewed life that comes after we accept our powerlessness is full of possibilities—and a serenity we didn't
know before.

*Today I am grateful for the adult perspective I gained
from acknowledging a reality that I could not control.*

Not all who wander are lost.

—J. R. R. Tolkien

We are wandering on a path. We are able to look back and see how far we have come, and perhaps we can see some distance ahead. But we are exploring what a recovered life means. We cannot predict what will happen in the future, and we cannot see what is around the next bend. Some people respond to the unknown with fear. On the spiritual path we are following, we put fear in our back pocket. We continue to wander while practicing the principle of turning our lives and our will over to the care of God. There is no need to fear. We know that we will face challenges and we will not be alone.

Since we cannot foresee what will happen in the future, we can only know that we will meet whatever happens with our best self. Life is an adventure. The difference between fear and excitement is the knowledge that our Higher Power will be with us. We have our friends; we have our honesty and our self-respect. Even though we don't know what is around the next turn, we are not lost.

Today I am grateful to be in the care of my Higher Power.

We do not err because truth is difficult to see. It is visible at a glance. We err because this is more comfortable.

—Alexander Solzhenitsyn

When we are directed to make a "searching and fearless" moral inventory of ourselves, it is because in our old ways we looked for the more comfortable answers. Honesty with ourselves can be uncomfortable when we first let ourselves in on the secrets we kept away from our consciousness. We see things we do not want to look at. We may have long-held patterns of shaping and softening the facts so we could continue our harmful and self-abusive ways. And as we lied to and betrayed ourselves, we made ourselves weaker and less able to deal with our situation.

Now we value honesty with ourselves. Honesty may be uncomfortable, but it will not hurt us. Once we have the courage to be honest with ourselves, we don't have to decide immediately what we will do with what we see. We can take it in steps. First we admit what we know to be true—and then we can live with what we know for a while. Slowly wisdom will grow within us and we will more clearly see a path for how to proceed.

Today I will not shy away from honesty with myself.

The fastest way to freedom is to feel your feelings.

—Gita Bellin

Many of us were taught in boyhood that feelings should be avoided. Some men think that any kind of vulnerability should be hidden, and most feelings can make us feel vulnerable. For some of us, the only acceptable feeling is the one that makes us feel stronger: anger. Many men don't even know what their feelings are; many others recognize their feelings but have never learned how to express them to others. When we found our addictions and codependencies, they quickly became handy ways to hide from feelings. But that only served our false sense of masculinity.

As we seek a life free from compulsions and addictions, moving from the foolish ways to the wise ways of true manhood, we honestly admit our feelings. We are strong enough to stop hiding. We honestly feel our feelings because they allow us to live more fully.

Today I will be conscious of my feelings and give them a place in my life.

I felt angry toward my friend.
I told my wrath. My wrath did end.
I felt angry toward my foe.
I told him not. My wrath did grow.

—William Blake

A basic fact of our human nature is that expressing our feelings helps resolve them. When we push them down or keep them hidden, we preserve them and save them up, and sometimes the pressure only makes them grow. Many of us are afraid that expressing our feelings will make things worse. We have learned that we are capable of suppressing our feelings to smooth situations over. However, those feelings come out later, either through uncontrolled outrage or as problems with our health.

A good relationship only grows deeper and more trusting when we express our feelings to each other. It may feel awkward or risky to tell a loved one that we feel hurt, but when we say it respectfully, we can expect a respectful reply. When we have good methods of communication, our relationships grow stronger and deeper with each passing year.

When I feel anger, I will express it respectfully.

In everyone's heart stirs a great homesickness.

—Rabbi Seymour Siegel

We ask ourselves, what drove us to do some of the things we did? We went to extremes when we knew our actions were not rational. Even today, we are drawn to extremes. At times we still long for things that we know will hurt us. Are we puzzled by these desires?

Wise men and prophets have searched their own deep truths to understand their desires and longings. Many say that our desires and hungers are, at the base of our being, a search for a spiritual home, a place where we know we are welcome, safe, and loved. Perhaps we are all born longing for that home. Maybe we first taste it when we first experience the warmth of loving and caring parents, even when it was only a taste, and only partially satisfied. Then we spend the rest of our lives in pursuit of that good feeling again.

The wisdom of the Twelve Steps points us toward that spiritual home. A lifetime of growth and development follows in which we feel the spirit in our fellowship with other men and women, and we learn from others how they have found their way home.

Today the stirring in my heart will be a sign of my spiritual longing.

When the truth is told lovingly, with insight and compassion, you can say anything.

—Shawnee Undell

There are times when we know something, or we have a difficult thing to say to someone, and we can't see how we could possibly speak it. Perhaps today our spouse or dear friend has done something we feel upset about, or perhaps someone at work is doing something that we need to discuss with him or her.

When we have a hard message to deliver, we don't have to speak it harshly. We can say almost anything to someone if we can put our arm around that person, figuratively speaking. Naturally, we can't always expect to be received with open arms when our message is hard to hear. A sensitive or painful truth sometimes is the valuable gift that only we as friends can deliver. We don't even have to be right; what is required it that we are sincere.

Today I will look for loving and compassionate ways to say my truth.

> *To the rationally minded, the mental processes of the*
> *intuitive appear to work backward. His conclusions are*
> *reached before his premises.*
>
> —Frances Wickes

Intuition is a valuable form of wisdom that often seems mystical. We lose our keys and can't find them in any of the usual places and then an idea pops into our mind about where to find them. When we look there, we find them. Only after the fact can we explain— maybe—why that spot came to mind. That's intuition. Or, on a higher plane, we have a feeling that a certain choice in our life would be a big mistake, or one day, for no clear reason, we expect our partner to tell us something important.

The wisdom of our intuition deserves our great respect. It is a valuable guide. Even though it is not 100 percent accurate, and we cannot expect it to be, we should not violate ourselves by contradicting it. Instead, we grow by developing our intuition, listening to what we imagine and what we feel, and following our instincts. Intuition is another form of spiritual strength.

Today I will listen to my inner feelings about things,
even when I don't immediately understand them
rationally.

Life is what happens to you when you're busy making other plans.

—John Lennon

We have plans and dreams about our future. We hope to accomplish certain goals in our lives. Maybe we want to buy a house or get a promotion. We have a future with our life partner, or we are looking for a life partner. But life is never so cut-and-dried that we should expect everything to go according to our plans. We live better and healthier if we hold loosely to our anticipations; the path we walk in reality isn't ever the exact path we envisioned. Life is an adventure in which sometimes things turn out even better than we hoped, and sometimes we have to cope with great disappointments.

Surprisingly, after we deal with the unexpected, we are often grateful for what it brought or what we learned. How often have we heard someone say he is grateful for the way an illness changed his life, or the way a great loss taught him to be a better person? Perhaps today we have to face a difficult challenge or manage a problem that we would never have chosen. The difficulty that we face is part of our unique life journey, and if we allow it to, it will guide us toward becoming a better man.

Today I will make my plans and still be willing to deal with whatever happens.

When a man's willing and eager, the gods join in.

—Aeschylus

We can learn a lot about our present state of mind by asking ourselves what we are willing and eager for. Just now, are we willing to know ourselves better? Do we seek to become better human beings? Are we willing to move beyond self-destructive desires and leave them behind? Or are we more willing and eager for someone else to make things easy for us? Are we still holding on to our desires for control? Do we still hold on to hope for another ecstatic high?

After we face ourselves with the truth of what we really want, the truth can change us. First we are honest with ourselves, and that boosts our ability to actively choose what we really want. When we become willing, we are ready for the work of our Higher Power to help us go where we want to go.

Today I will keep in mind what I really want and not become distracted by temptations that lead off the path.

Loss is another word for change.

—M. Tating

We don't always realize how loss and grief are natural parts of life. Every change contains a loss within it. If we get a job promotion, we lose some elements of our work that are familiar and maybe enjoyable. If we get married, we lose the independence of the single life. If we choose recovery, we lose the friends we had in our addiction and codependency. And, of course, when we lose a loved one, the changes that follow are never chosen, but they may actually lead us toward new possibilities.

Surprisingly, every loss, every grief, has embedded within it the gift of a new beginning. In the midst of our losses, we can seldom see the gift. We don't want to lose what we love. And grief is a necessary part of letting go. Grief is the wail of pain that comes when we know we must let go. And then life goes on. There is life after loss! It is a changed life. Perhaps nothing will ever be the same as it was. But it can become a new stage of our life, deeper and richer, even though we never could have imagined it.

Today I embrace change, even knowing it means some loss.

A word from the heart goes straight to the heart.

—Abbe Huvelin

When we have something important to tell someone, we may feel afraid of how it will be received. Or when a friend experiences a tragedy, we may wonder what to say: this kind of situation can throw us into retreat mode and leave us silent. Or maybe we carry secrets we wish we could share, but we don't dare to speak. It's reassuring to recall the times when people have said important things to us. Their sincerity always meant more than any particular words they used.

Our message always contains more than just words. The very fact that we let someone into our confidence is a compliment. The fact that we care enough to show our feelings is a message of trust. When we give that kind of compliment to someone, we have a right to expect it to be treated gently, as a gift.

Today, in my personal relationships, I will speak from my heart.

Life is a great big canvas, and you should throw all the paint on it you can.

—Danny Kaye

Our recovery started because of unmanageability and loss of control. That was a very frightening state of life. However, if simply abstaining was our entire goal, we would become very suppressed and limited beings. Our need for caution and control would become pervasive in our lives. That is where a dry drunk is stuck. A successful and happy recovery brings freedom, peace of mind, and self-esteem. We learn how to relax and enjoy life to its fullest because we no longer have to be so concerned with control. We can release our deeper selves to engage freely in the wholesome and healthy pleasure of friendships, love and sex, family connections, good food, sports and recreation, and fulfilling work.

We don't have to hold back our enthusiasm for life any longer. We are free to release our playfulness and take risks because we have a safe base in our Higher Power and our program. We can imagine trips we want to take, we can let our intuition speak to us, and we can dream of things we want to do and make plans to fulfill them.

Today I will paint freely on the canvas before me.

To have more, desire less.

—*Table Talk*

So many of us are caught up in such a busy pace of life that we feel we don't have time for the basic things like dinner with our family, time to talk to our intimate partner, or quiet time to unwind and reflect. What is the problem? Often the problem is that we are caught in a never-ending search for more material things than our income can comfortably afford. In modern life, we are daily subjected to well-crafted advertising that tells us we would be happy if we bought another alluring item. Turning aside from those seductions, deciding we can live more comfortably if we seek happiness elsewhere, frees us from that demanding cycle.

If we examine our desires, we will quickly recognize that we already have enough material goods. Happiness, gratitude, and peace of mind will come from the abundance of our relationships and the knowledge that we are the kind of men we hope to be. We can limit our desires for more goods and free ourselves from the feeling that we don't have enough.

Today I will remind myself that I have enough. I am grateful for the abundance in my life.

*A great teacher never strives to explain his vision—
he simply invites you to stand beside him and see for
yourself.*

—Reverend R. Inman

In the spirit of our recovering fellowship, we are very
cautious about advising anyone. Advice is only given
when requested and even then with great care. Words
of advice are so easily spoken but so often off target.
We all find it easy to see what someone else should do,
but the much harder task is to find insight into our
own actions. So we focus on the harder and more helpful part, striving to live our lives as well as possible. We
can grow by standing beside other successful recovering people and learning how they do it, and we can
allow others to stand beside us to learn what they can.

A good example is always the best teacher. The wisest men are not sure their advice is useful to anyone.
They just live their lives in ways that suit them, and
others can take from it whatever is useful and leave
the rest.

*Today I will work on the harder task of deepening my
insight into my own thoughts and actions.*

Do not let a little dispute injure a great friendship.

—H. Jackson Brown, Jr.

There are many kinds of friends. Some are work friends; we enjoy knowing each other and doing our jobs but don't ever get very personal. We have recreational friends with whom we enjoy doing the same activities. Some friends are like soul mates; we feel we were cut from the same cloth and we understand each other at a deep level. With our soul mates we can talk about almost anything—and sometimes we don't have to talk about it. And some friends are lifelong buddies who knew us way back when; we know each other in ways that new friends never can.

Our egos can get in the way and spoil the development of good friendships. For instance, we may take things too personally and feel offended over small things. Or sometimes our ego may be so determined to be right that we sacrifice the friendship in order to stand up for our position. A good friendship requires that our ego step back a bit, making room for others to have dignity and be imperfect too.

Today I am grateful for all the different kinds of friends in my life.

A man of faith does not bargain or stipulate with God.
—Mahatma Gandhi

When we finally admitted that we were powerless over the substance or behavior of our addiction or codependency, we had already covered a lot of ground. Most of us had suffered great personal despair, defeat, and self-hate before we could see our problem for what it was. As the Big Book of Alcoholics Anonymous says, we, too, had "tried to find easier and softer ways, but we could not." We bargained with ourselves and with nature, saying we would cut back or we would abstain for a period of time. Nothing short of total, unconditional acceptance of our powerlessness could release us from the grips of our problem.

The paradox of this surrender to reality didn't strike us until later. Surrender to the truth is liberating. As long as we admit our powerlessness daily and never again try to bargain ourselves into a position of control, we are free to become the kind of men we respect and to have the respect of those we love.

Today, once again, as if for the first time, I admit my powerlessness and throw myself on the grace of my Higher Power to restore my spirit.

I'm as pure as the driven slush.

—Tallulah Bankhead

There is something to be said for claiming our imperfection and wearing it proudly. There is so much more freedom and health in imperfection than in the stifling and unreal drive to be perfect. When we decide to put the shame and dishonor of our misbehaviors behind us, we are tempted to think that the opposite extreme would be better, but it is not. Instead of striving to be perfect, let us accept our imperfection. Instead of trying to climb to the top of the ladder of perfect actions, let us accept that we will make mistakes and that no honest man will ever reach that point. Let us strive instead to keep returning to our standards.

Many of us have said that living one day at a time is too much for us. We tell ourselves that we are just going to live this day, but a half hour later we are worrying again about the future. We have to keep reminding ourselves to live one minute or one hour at a time. That is the attitude we adopt when we accept our imperfection. Instead of expecting to hold to our standards perfectly, we simply keep returning to them.

Today I embrace my imperfection, and when I veer off course, I will keep returning to my path.

> *It is well to remind ourselves that anxiety signifies*
> *a conflict, and so long as a conflict is going on, a*
> *constructive solution is possible.*
>
> —Rollo May

Anxiety is a sign of life. All living things experience it; it is nothing to be feared. In fact, we double our anxiety if we are afraid of our feelings of fear. Anxious feelings may be a guide, an intuition pointing us in a direction we need to follow. They can direct us away from some situations and toward others. They may be a sign that we have neglected something or that an important matter remains unfinished.

When we become familiar with our feelings, we also become more comfortable with them. We welcome them like friends who tell us what we need to pay attention to. One way to become more aware of our feelings is to just pause and quietly breathe with slow, deep breaths. In that simple physical act, our bodies quiet down and we can think more clearly.

> *Today I will give my anxiety its rightful place rather*
> *than fighting it, and I will pay attention to its message.*

Baseball teaches us, or has taught most of us, how to deal with failure. We learn at a very young age that failure is the norm in baseball and . . . errors [are] part of the game, part of its rigorous truth.

—Francis T. Vincent, Jr.

Of course we will make mistakes. We are born with the right to make mistakes. There is no shame in that. Perfection is a false ideal for a real human being. We learn by trial and error. If we try to be perfect, we will meet dead ends and roadblocks because we will inevitably fall short.

Instead, there is wisdom in the motto, "Keep coming back." In this instance, the motto refers to returning to our standards. Rather than to strive constantly for higher and higher perfection, our goal is to always return to the rules we live by. Of course we will veer off the path. When we do, we make repairs, pay our dues, and hold our place as full-fledged members of the human race.

Today my goal is to keep returning to my ethics for a good life.

I've had a wonderful time but this wasn't it.

—Groucho Marx

How often we went out in search of pleasure to escape our problems, and our desires only led us into much bigger problems. Alcohol, gambling, sex, food, and even taking care of others are all pleasures. They have been part of good times in many people's lives. But we know that pursuit of these pleasures can be abused and create only heartache and sickness.

In this program we are dealing with the age-old problem of how to manage our desires. This is a spiritual problem. We are born with desires. Our development into strong manhood is partly a growth in our ability to learn from experience and choose how and when to satisfy these desires—and which ones are best left unsatisfied. We are learning that a hearty, healthy man can live very well with some desires unfulfilled.

Today I will have a wonderful time, in part, because I choose to leave some desires and impulses unsatisfied.

*But they that wait upon the Lord shall renew their
strength; they shall mount up with wings as eagles; they
shall run, and not be weary; and they shall walk, and
not faint.*

—Isaiah 40:31

The Third Step tells us that the path of recovery includes a "decision to turn our will and our lives over to
the care of God *as we understood Him.*" The ancient
Hebrew text tells us poetically that wonderful things
happen in our lives when we take this spiritual Step.
We enter a paradox: turning our lives and will over to
the care of our Higher Power in fact inspires us with
greater strength.

Our own life stories, and the stories of healing and
recovery that we hear from our friends and our mentors, illustrate this biblical wisdom. Our lives were a
mess. We tried to control more than a man can control
and we ended up out of control. The losses we paid
were painful and heartbreaking. But when we chose to
enter into a spiritual recovery, we felt we had rejoined
the human family. We were inspired with a new sense
of hope and energy and possibilities for our lives.

*Today, again, I turn to my Higher Power for the care
of my life and my will.*

*It is perfectly true, as philosophers say, that life must
be understood backwards. But they forget the other
proposition, that it must be lived forwards.*

—Søren Kierkegaard

Real life presents us with unexpected puzzles and challenges. Like going on a trip, part of the reason for going
is to experience the unexpected. Looking forward on
our path, we see bends and turns ahead and we don't
know what's around them. So we look forward to them
with a mixture of anticipation and concern.

This adventure of life deepens with the understanding we get from our past experiences. What we have already learned sharpens our skills for dealing with
today, and still we will meet new surprises, and we will
continue to learn. Even though we have no control
over what appears on our path, there is no need for
fear or panic because we have turned our lives over to
the care of our Higher Power. We will learn how to deal
with it.

*Today I rely on what I have learned about life, and
I trust in God to support me.*

*We only have one person to blame, and that's
each other.*

—Barry Beck, NHL player

Blame is not a word that works well for us. It is an attack word, a negative assault that fails to point toward
anything better. Much better is the word *responsible*.
When a man opens a door and accidentally knocks
down a child on the other side, he is responsible for his
action, and he reaches down to help the child up again.
It is nothing to be ashamed of or blamed for. He isn't a
bad person for doing that. But he takes responsibility.

Blame and responsibility are difficult matters for us
to separate. Many of us have felt blamed and shamed
from our earliest memories. As a result, when we are responsible, we have a knee-jerk impulse to feel ashamed.
But taking responsibility without shame is what a
strong man does. We can learn to separate them, and
as we do, our self-esteem rises.

*Today I will take responsibility for my actions and
respect myself for doing so.*

The man who has no imagination has no wings.

—Muhammad Ali

The most important creative project we have is our own lives, and imagination is a rich inner resource to guide us. We can develop our imagination if we give ourselves permission to dream and to let go of the bonds of reality and our immediate situation.

If I could be anywhere in the world right now, where would I want to be? What would I be doing? Who would be there with me? If I took a break from all my responsibilities for a day, what would I do with the day? What is it like to be another person, such as my best friend, my boss, my child? How would I most like to celebrate my next birthday? If today were the last day of my life, how would I want to live this day? If I could accomplish only one more thing in my life, what would I choose?

Today I will let my thoughts take wing and fly into the creative world of imagination.

July

□ □ □ □ □ □ □

*The past has flown away. The coming month and year
do not exist; ours only is the present's tiny point.*

—Shabestari

We are tempted to look back and to look ahead. But
what we most need to do is be present in this moment, with ourselves, with our loved ones and friends,
and with our experience right here and right now.
When we were lost and asleep in our using days and
codependency, we could not be emotionally present.
Our thoughts were taken up with how we would get
our next drink, our next big gambling win, or our next
sexual exploit—or with how to handle the latest crisis.
To be emotionally present and live in the moment:
this takes time, and it's a frame of mind that develops
as we grow in recovery.

One way we become more present in the moment is
to practice gratitude. We can always name a few things
we feel grateful for: small and big things, funny and serious things. Looking through the lens of gratitude
brings us into the immediate moment.

*Today I will look at my day through the lens of
gratitude.*

My life is in the hands of any fool who makes me lose my temper.

—Joseph Hunter

Many of us have learned that we can get a real buzz from anger. It seems to give us direct access to our egos, where we feel an inflated sense of power and entitlement. We no longer feel vulnerable; we see things in black and white terms. We believe we are right. But in this primitive state of excitement, we are reacting from the animal level, and our grown-up brain has been bypassed. This kind of habitual reaction can leave a lot of damage in its aftermath. It undermines our dearest relationships and our own self-respect.

We need to examine our patterns with anger. We don't seek to be rid of it but to manage it as grown men. Do we take responsibility for staying honest in the midst of anger? Can we hold onto our humility while being angry? When we express angry feelings, do we avoid abusive words and intimidating actions? We can feel our anger and express it without reverting to our primitive brain.

Today I will be aware of angry feelings and express them with a clear sense of my grown-up masculinity.

To err is human; to blame it on the other guy is even more human.

—Bob Goddard

We are on a path that leads us to become better men with greater insight and stronger character. A central theme on this path is learning to take responsibility for ourselves, our mistakes, and our choices as we deal with our situation. We can make progress on this path by noticing our defensive reactions when we make a mistake or when someone criticizes us. Our old ways were aimed at shifting the blame or counterattacking to get someone else off our case. Now we are learning how to take on the blame when it honestly belongs to us.

One of the first things we need to learn in taking responsibility is that there is no shame in making a mistake. Everyone makes mistakes. But some people don't accept responsibility for them, and others do. We have much greater respect for someone who does. Admitting when we were wrong doesn't mean speaking in vague generalities, saying that "mistakes were made." It doesn't mean saying, "Yes, I did this, but only because you did that." It means saying what we did or didn't do and laying the facts out there for us and others to deal with. When we can do that, forgiveness almost always follows shortly.

Today I will hold back my defensiveness and admit the facts as they are.

*A community is like a ship, everyone ought to be
prepared to take the helm.*

—Henrik Ibsen

A good life is blessed with many communities. There
are neighborhoods, schools, synagogues, churches,
mosques, groups of friends, workplaces, and Twelve
Step recovery groups. We became alienated from our
communities when we were attached to our addictions
and codependency. The all-consuming demands of our
misguided lives left little room for genuine participation in the human network.

On our path, we now treasure these connections.
We are participants in the bonds of warmth and the
many good relationships that surround us. We don't
have to be the center of attention or the main focus in
order to feel included. We contribute to the networks
that we are part of by simply being good men, and by
taking our share of the duties that make a better community for us all.

*Today I will seek to make a positive contribution to the
communities in my life.*

Some people are so afraid to die that they never begin to live.

—Henry Van Dyke

Fear is a dirty word for most guys. We find it hard to admit the truth. But the truth is, in our denial of fear we have often been ruled by it. We certainly know the fear of going without the comfort we had in our addictive and codependent ways. Our anxiety was hidden under our controlling behaviors when we said, "I'm only doing it because I love you," or "I'm only going to take a little hit." Many of us have felt so alone and grew up in such a stressful world that we learned to be constantly on guard against danger, even as we denied our fears.

Life inherently involves risk. There is such a thing as too much control. In its ultimate form, control is static and dead. That is why spiritual awakening is so central to our healing and recovery. We can stay spiritually alive, aware of life's risks but remaining calm. When we fear what this day will bring, or what the future holds, we place our fears in the hands of God as we understand God. What happens next is beyond rational explanation, but it lets us go forward without grasping for our old self-destructive comforts.

Today I will admit that I feel fear as any man does, and I stay calm in the care of God.

You're never too old to grow up.

—Shirley Conran

A child's view of adults is that they have arrived at some fixed point where they are emancipated and have all the tools necessary for life. An adult knows that we never stop growing. Many of us have been stuck in an immature level of development. Our life stresses and our addictions took us off the track of emotional growth. We found substitutes and evasions for truly dealing with the normal life problems. Now we are back on the much more rewarding path of truly living and growing.

We accept the adult wisdom that we all need help and we all continue to learn and grow throughout our life span. We finally feel like adults because we take responsibility for our actions. We don't blame others for our problems, and when our days feel challenging, we can ask for help. Back on our path, we are never alone.

Today I am grateful to be on the path of dealing with my life and continuing to grow truly stronger.

It is the wounded oyster that mends its shell with pearl.

—Ralph Waldo Emerson

Many of us felt like outsiders in the past. As children we weren't in the most popular group, or we were picked last when teams were chosen. And almost everyone has been picked on sometimes. As adults our wounds may have been self-inflicted, but no less painful for that. The key question today is, are we still on a track that creates more wounds, or are we on the mend?

There is great spiritual benefit to knowing what it feels like to be a wounded person. It provides the resource that many great men have built their wisdom and perspective upon. We all know men we admire deeply who have come through hard and painful times, not knowing how it would all turn out. They followed this path of healing and spiritual growth and, because of their healing, have become men of the highest quality.

Today I can see my past wounds as a source for spiritual and emotional strength.

*Victory is in the quality of competition, not the
final score.*

—Mike Marshall

Competition is neither good nor bad. It is like any
other force that can be used in good ways or bad. For
us, winning means being the kind of man we most admire. When we are in a competitive game, whether it is
in athletics, business, or a friendly discussion, we strive
first to compete in ways that we respect. We don't give
up our moral or human values in order to come out
with the top score at the end. We don't indulge in hate
or anger at the other guy simply because he is our competition at the moment. We play fair, we respect others,
and we enjoy a good and worthy competitor.

Keeping our eye on the ball means we stay focused
on what we are truly trying to win. That is a kind of wisdom that we weren't born with; we develop it through
conscious effort and attention. Today we certainly face
some competitive situations, whether it is engaging
with a particular co-worker or someone with an oppos-
ing viewpoint in a group we are part of. At the end of
the day, if we have our values intact, we will have won
our best prize.

Today I will be a strong and honorable competitor.

Don't go around saying the world owes you a living.
The world owes you nothing. It was here first.

—Mark Twain

Some men have a very passive attitude about their life. While they may seem to have a lot of bravado, they feel dependent on the inside and look to others to supply what they need. When it doesn't come, they feel hurt, neglected, and angry. Others see their life as a gift from the beginning. Opportunities may be more or less available, but they use what they have to create a life that has meaning. They don't settle for negative thinking and they develop a rewarding inner world.

We can change our attitude toward our lives. All of us have some unproductive, negative thoughts that only keep us stuck. Perhaps we have old resentments that burden our days, or we hold on to old debts that could never be repaid. To free ourselves to live fully, we can consciously and deliberately reshape these thoughts. We can shift our attention from what we don't have to what is possible now.

Today I am grateful for the gift of life, and I will take
my life and grow from here.

The significant problems we face cannot be solved at the same level of thinking we were at when we created them.

—Albert Einstein

Many of us stubbornly hold on to our long-established, preferred ways of looking at things. We don't think we are stubborn, only that we rely on what worked for us in the past. Perhaps as young guys we coped with stress by keeping our thoughts to ourselves, or we figured out that we wouldn't get hurt if we didn't trust anyone. All of the patterns that we developed as youngsters were our best attempts at the time to deal with our lives. The greater the stress we felt, the harder won were our coping responses, and the stronger our attachment to them.

Our best answers from boyhood may not fit our lifetimes as men. Holding too dearly to childhood solutions freezes us in immature and weaker levels of growth. What was charming and harmless behavior in a child can be manipulating and dishonest in a man. Thus we create new problems. We need to let ourselves become more vulnerable—to give up the security of our old ways and open ourselves to the messages coming from our friends, our program, and our experiences.

Today I will be open to insecurity and create the possibility of growing stronger.

We couldn't conceive of a miracle if none had ever happened.

—Libbie Fudim

We are very familiar with miracles. We see the change that has happened in our own lives and in the lives of others on this journey with us. Something deep within us changed when we first decided we could accept the truth of our powerlessness and the help of a Higher Power. When a man's personality changes profoundly, that is a miracle.

These transformations go beyond what anyone might rationally expect. Some of us had given up and were without hope. Others had given up on us too. We thought our lives could never be different after we lived so long in the grips of codependency and addiction, after we tried in so many ways to manage and control our actions and repeatedly failed. But this program provided an awakening, as if from a deep sleep or perhaps a nightmare. Now we have found a path that produces genuine miracles. We cannot easily explain it, but our compulsions are lifted.

Today I am grateful for the miracle in my own life and the lives of my friends.

Before talking of holy things, we prepare ourselves by offering . . . One will fill his pipe and hand it to the other who will light it and offer it to the sky and the earth . . . They will smoke together . . . Then we will be ready to talk.

—Mato-Kuwapi, Santee Yankton Sioux

Rituals prepare us for moments of spiritual experience. They bring people together; they mark occasions; they give us metaphors through our senses that expose us to mystery, awe, peace, and wisdom. Traditional spiritual practices all use ritual to reach toward God. In our meetings we also have rituals that accomplish these things.

We may have dismissed ritual in our cynical minds, thinking of it as irrelevant hocus-pocus. But when we seek connection with other people, or with God, we learn that ritual is a way to set our cynical minds aside and open ourselves to the presence. Even in our private time of prayer and meditation, we may light a candle as a sign of our spiritual search.

Today I will honor the rituals that create conscious contact.

I don't ask for the meaning of the song of a bird or the rising of the sun on a misty morning. There they are, and they are beautiful.

—Pete Hamill

Nature is the mystical, spiritual miracle present all around us every day. A walk in the woods or a hike in a park provides us with abundant evidence that we are part of something much bigger than ourselves. No one sent the bird to sing its song; no person designed a tree and planned its leaves to come forth. They are just doing their own thing. Our whole world is generously decorated by spontaneous beauty, and our senses take them in at no cost.

When we feel burdened by our problems and when we are too focused on ourselves, a walk outdoors will surely lighten the load. We can feel the wind in our face, look up at the sky and see the big and ever-changing heavens, or lie on the ground and feel the support of the earth. It is always a good practice to turn to the natural world when we feel the need for spiritual refreshment.

Today I will get outside myself by noticing the eternal world of nature.

> *How much more grievous are the consequences of*
> *anger than the causes of it.*

—Marcus Aurelius

Anger shatters our calm. Some of us show it in loud bursts; others just quietly stew. Sometimes we feel angry inside but we still want to look kind and unperturbed, so our anger comes out sideways, hurting someone indirectly or in sneaky ways. We all have felt the pangs of regret after we said or did something in anger. We wish we could magically turn back the clock and undo the moment, gather up the pieces, and put them back together again.

No one can simply banish the basic human emotion of anger from his life. To be responsible, we must accept our anger. It arises from within us and handling it is our own responsibility, even when we are perfectly justified in feeling angry. We choose our way to express it. It is never responsible to say, "You made me angry, so it's your fault that I blew up."

After accepting our anger we strive to develop a space between the feeling and our actions. We learn to notice our feelings before they reach the explosion point. In that mental space we choose how to express them.

> *Today I will notice and accept my anger, then choose*
> *respectful ways to express it.*

We haven't needed to direct our minds consciously all that much until now, and we haven't really understood the delicacy and absolute necessity of doing so— until now.

—Robert Ornstein

When we are highly alert to this very moment and we feel the importance of focusing our conscious minds, we are in a spiritual space. Our spiritual development grows along these lines—we become more and more skilled at centering our senses and our consciousness in this moment. This is how our calmness and serenity grow.

We know that our health and survival depend upon our spiritual growth. It is urgent for us, and for those that we love, that we become better, more serene men. We can practice this by always being mindful of the concrete truths around us, and by doing just one thing at a time. When we eat, we are aware of the flavors and textures of our food. When we wash the dishes, we focus our mind on just washing the dishes. Multitasking does not advance our spiritual growth or serenity. Calmness comes when we focus our minds and allow all distractions to fall away.

Today is the day I am alive, and in this day I will practice focusing my consciousness.

Man is harder than iron, stronger than stone and more fragile than a rose.

—Turkish proverb

It is a boy's idea of a real man that leaves no room for softness or weakness. In his view, a real man is either strong or weak, either tough or soft. But a boy is not yet a man, and he can only imitate grown men. As we develop into adults with real life experience, and as we get to know ourselves with honesty, we no longer have to view our masculinity as a caricature. We know that our true nature contains both toughness and gentleness. When we are at peace with ourselves, we don't have to hide our gentleness to prove that we are strong.

We no longer have to prove anything. We have self-acceptance, including the whole complex mixture of elements that make up our character. And with self-acceptance, we don't need to focus on the image we portray to others. We just let ourselves be and express the truth of how we feel and who we are. That is the sign of a real man who has grown up.

Today I am growing in self-knowledge and I accept myself as a complex mixture.

Courage is the price that life exacts for granting peace.
—Amelia Earhart

Courage is a traditional masculine virtue. We admire a man who bravely faces danger and does battle for a worthy cause. When courage fails a man, when he steps aside from the battle that needs to be fought, we feel that he missed his calling.

Recovery requires this kind of courage. In fact, the struggles with ourselves and with our inner demons are far more frightening than duking it out with a real live foe. We might get a thrill from the danger of driving fast, or climbing a rock wall, or skiing a challenging slope, yet we freeze when we try to talk about our feelings or make amends for a bad mistake.

The very act of beginning our recovery took courage. We put it off as long as we could. The battle seemed so frightening. When we could see no other escape, we raised the courage to go forward toward a worthwhile goal. And the peace that we have now is the reward for our courage.

Today I pray for the courage to do what I am called to do.

The mind creates the abyss and the heart crosses it.

—Nisargadatta Maharaj

Sometimes we are filled with fear. The challenges facing us seem so large and we feel so confused or so stymied. We wake in the middle of the night and the worst images rise up in our thoughts. Our problems, real or imagined, can overwhelm us. We feel bereft and alone.

Yet, honestly, we don't have to live the whole future in one day, and we don't have to deal with everything alone. When running a long distance, we may feel tired and can't imagine continuing to the end. Yet we know we can keep running now, and we can keep taking step after step. We don't have to expend all of our energy in one burst. Our energy rebuilds along the path, even as we expend it. So it is with meeting the challenges of our lives. We take heart in knowing that we only have to deal with today. We are never alone because our creator is always with us.

Today I will cross over any difficulty I must face.

Eternity is a terrible thought. I mean, where's it going to end?

—Tom Stoppard

Looking at the stars on a clear night or the vastness of the open sea gives us a sense of how small we are. It may feel frightening to contemplate—and at the same time comforting. What are we but a bit of earth sparked to life by a force we didn't initiate? This rich mixture of fear, comfort, and awe is what we can call spirituality.

In our program of recovery, we are guided to a spiritual path. The very search for a sense of meaning is a spiritual quest. We are told to have faith in the God of our understanding, and the paradox is that God is beyond our understanding. God exceeds the confines of a human definition. When we can relax into that realization, we find comfort in the vastness and we focus on being the best kind of man we know how to be.

I can be at peace, knowing that what is eternal exceeds my understanding.

The trouble with not having a goal is that you can
spend your life running up and down the field and
never scoring.

—Bill Copeland

We all have goals. Some of them are implicit or even
beneath our conscious awareness. Some of us have very
clear goals that we have spelled out for ourselves.
Perhaps we are seeking to hold a certain job some day.
Maybe we have the goal of saving money for our children's college fund. Another goal might be to complete
a particular next Step in our recovery program.

It helps to spell out a few goals that we truly want to
accomplish. Sitting down and writing just a few goals
helps us find direction. That kind of list is best when it
is kept short, limited to a few things we sincerely care
about. Then we have a focus to inform our small and
large daily decisions.

Today I will think about my goals so that I can be
clearer about how to achieve them.

Prayer is less about changing the world than it is about changing ourselves.

—David J. Wolpe

Regardless of how we understand a Power greater than ourselves, prayer is an important part of our lives. Relating to a Higher Power leads us out of our egotism into a conscious relationship with powers far beyond ourselves.

How do we pray? We can use words to state what's on our mind. We can say them silently or out loud. We can quiet our mind and simply enter into the peace of God, opening our mind to receive that deeper wisdom. Drawing pictures can be a form of prayer. Playing music or listening to music can be done prayerfully. This is not so much a time to ask for special favors as a time to enter the relationship and to receive the guidance that comes from beyond our own power and conscious will.

Today I will quiet my mind for a few minutes and enter consciously into a prayerful relationship with my Higher Power.

I not only bow to the inevitable; I am fortified by it.
                                        —Thornton Wilder

Some people understand great wisdom naturally without a struggle. Most of us have endured great pain and
saw our lives career out of control before we were willing to admit that we could be powerless. We wanted
our pleasures and our escapes and we did not want to
conform to the truth. Our stories illustrate what happened when we refused to accept reality.

Now we also see how much stronger we become
when we accept the wisdom of humility. When we put
aside our hungry egos and bow to the inevitable truth,
we begin to work with reality instead of against it. Our
transformed lives are miracles because they grew from
such out-of-control lives so filled with mistakes.

*Today I am grateful for the humility and wisdom that
has fortified me.*

Man needs difficulties; they are necessary for health.

                                  —Carl Jung

When we are in the midst of problems and stresses, we can gather great strength from looking back at how far we have already come. True maturity gives us the perspective to see the bigger picture and to know that our present problems and distress will heal and pass into the background. At the same time, we can see from looking back that the obstacles we faced have changed us, and we have become stronger and better men as a result.

Today's obstacles, whether large or small, call us to bring our best wisdom in meeting them. We cannot foresee exactly how successful we will be. But we can resolve to be the best kind of man we know how to be, with honesty and gentleness. And that is a success we can guarantee.

Today I will meet the obstacles I face with all the maturity I've got and with the strength of my honesty.

*When the mind is still . . . it returns to itself, and
by means of itself ascends to the thought of God.*

—Saint Basil the Great

Our path is not leading us toward a physical place but
toward the kind of person we are becoming. The
Twelve Steps guide us to use daily meditation as a tool
that helps us shape this new person. We take time for
quiet moments, we still our thoughts, and in the stillness, without effort, our minds naturally open to in-
troduce ourselves to ourselves. We become increasingly
honest with ourselves and some would say we hear the
voice of God.

Daily readings can set a calming tone. Then we take
a period of time, perhaps twenty minutes, for solitude
undisturbed by others or by distracting telephones or
television. We find that when we set aside this quiet
time, we actually seem to have more time, not less, for
the other demands in our lives.

*Today I will take a period of quiet time to come back
to myself.*

The pursuit of perfection often impedes improvement.
—George F. Will

When we are haunted by feelings of shame or self-loathing, anything less than perfection can remind us of those feelings. We seek straight A's and when we succeed, we feel that it was only barely good enough. Sometimes we may even avoid trying something new because we refuse to make the necessary mistakes involved. In contrast, it is said that Persian rug weavers, in the course of creating their stunningly beautiful carpets, deliberately weave at least one mistake into every rug so as to not compete with God.

We could all take a lesson for our lives from those weavers. On a day when we are overcome by anxiety about making a mistake, we can be more relaxed and more effective if we start out deliberately intending to make at least one mistake before the day is over. That way, we can make a place for imperfection and go on from there to do our best and learn from the experience.

Today I will make a place for imperfection and learn from my mistakes.

Your pain is the breaking of the shell that encloses your
understanding.

—Kahlil Gibran

We seldom choose the pain that comes into our lives.
Perhaps it comes as a consequence of other choices
that we made. Perhaps it comes as a result of events
that are no fault of our own. Either way, our suffering
is something we have no choice about. But we do have
choices about how we will respond to it. As men following a spiritual path, we have come to understand
that whatever we have to deal with contains important
lessons.

If a man falls and breaks his arm, no healing will
come from blaming the rock he stumbled over or
blaming the guy who put the rock in his way. He still
must care for his broken bone, and the healing comes
from within his own body.

We ask ourselves, what am I to learn from this
event? How can I take this experience and grow into a
better, stronger man? When we turn a painful thing
into a way to grow, we turn a negative to our advantage
and our lives take a turn for the better.

Today the pain I feel will point me in a direction for
my development.

*In running, it doesn't matter whether you come in first,
in the middle of the pack or last. You can say, "I have
finished." There is a lot of satisfaction in that.*

—Fred Lebow

In the ancient Greek competitions at Olympia, young
men came from all over the Greek nation to participate, and great honor was bestowed upon the winners.
But just to be a *participant,* in the Greek democratic
mind, was a high honor in itself.

We modern men sometimes lose that sense of true
honor. We think winning is the only goal. Such misguided beliefs have crippled us and made us feel like
losers. Have you ever watched wheelchair racers giving their all? These racers honor the true notion of
participation.

*Today I will participate with all of those around me,
to play, to run, and to work for a better world.*

*Sometimes I go about pitying myself, / and all the time /
I am being carried on great winds across the sky.*

—Ojibway song, translated by Frances Densmore,
adapted by Robert Bly

Self-pity is a rather silly temptation. Our troubles may
be very compelling and vivid. They may demand our attention. However, when we start to focus on ourselves
rather than our challenges, we get distracted from coping with them. Self-pity is a form of self-centeredness.
We think, *Why me?* or *Poor me,* or *Look at all the suffering I
have.* Whenever we let ourselves settle in on such self-
focused thinking, we become smaller men.

One way to move out of such a dead end is to laugh
at our narrowness. We can say, *There I go again, pitying
myself when there are so many blessings in life.* Another way
out is to look at our challenges as teachers and open
ourselves to learning their lessons.

*Today I will notice all the blessings that have brought
me this far in life and be open to the lessons that are
here for me to learn.*

Love is presence.

—Theresa Gerhardinger

When we sit with a loved one who is very ill, we often feel helpless. When a friend is confronted with great pain or tragedy, we wonder, *what should I say?* To be comfortable in any relationship, we need to understand powerlessness and accept it. Sometimes the only and the most loving thing to do is to be present.

When we see our wife or our partner make the same mistake over and over again, we want to take charge. When we don't get what we want from our beloved, we try to extract what we think we need. But we learn that true love exists within limits. We cannot fix others, and they cannot fix us. Once we accept the limits, once we accept powerlessness, we can relax into the love and enjoy its pleasures.

Today I will be present in the moment with the people in my life.

*Everything I did in my life that was worthwhile
I caught hell for.*

—Earl Warren

We have avoided conflict and sometimes taken the easier way when we should have stood up for what we believed in. We have procrastinated on difficult matters to keep the peace. Sometimes our fear of offending someone led us into dishonesty. We knew that if we said what we thought, or if we let others know our true feelings, we would have to deal with their reactions.

Great men do things that don't please everyone all the time. When we have true definition as a man, our boundaries will give others a target if they are looking for one. Perhaps, at work or at home, we have something we feel needs to be said but we know it will displease others. Even our Twelve Step meetings take inventory on what is going well and what is not. So we learn to stand up for our beliefs and our principles. If no one ever gives us hell, we are probably not doing our best.

Today I will act on my true beliefs and express my honest feelings.

Success is how high you bounce when you hit bottom.
—General George S. Patton

We all know about hitting bottom. Some of us look back and remember when we felt that we had lost everything. And some of us are grateful that we had a "high bottom." Either way, it is well for us to keep that memory close to us, because it is rich in lessons; hitting bottom motivated us to try something new. Our old patterns were broken and we were opened to new ways of living.

When the future seemed most bleak, we were finally able to accept a better way. Little did we know that this very moment was the dawning of great prospects for our lives. We are grateful not for the crisis itself, but for its lessons and our current recovery. The bounce that follows hitting bottom continues for a lifetime as we continue to become better men.

Today I am grateful for this path that leads out of my deep valley and on to new vistas.

August

□ □ □ □ □ □ □

*Hope has nothing to do with optimism. Its opposite is
not pessimism but despair.*

—William Sloane Coffin

Despair is the loss of all hope. We are all vulnerable to
slipping into that frame of mind at times. When our
troubles are at their worst, we may indulge in angry and
rebellious negative thinking. Such negative thinking is
basically self-centered and self-indulgent. At other
times we may feel that our lives are going well and we
have no good reason to despair, yet we lose our spirit
and vitality.

We can use our spiritual focus at these times to interrupt the negative thoughts. When we catch ourselves
thinking life is unfair and we are worthless, we can stop
following our thoughts down that track. Simply turning our attention elsewhere can help us restore our
spirit for life. This doesn't mean we fake optimism. It
means we choose to suspend our doubts and, just as we
might try on a new shirt, we try on the thought that we
are in the care of a Higher Power who accepts us as we
are. When we do that, a feeling of peace and calm will
follow.

*Today I will suspend feelings of despair and rest in the
faith that a Higher Power is present in my life.*

I've always wanted to be somebody, but I see now
I should have been more specific.

—Lily Tomlin

We are on an adult development journey. As we grow healthier, as we take our personal inventories, we develop into the kind of person we can respect and feel good about. From our addictive and codependent times, we know what it was like to feel empty—as if we were nobody. We had an exterior appearance of a whole person, but we were underdeveloped on the inside.

The promises of recovery always come true when we follow the steps toward honesty with ourselves and take responsibility for our actions. We may be assaulted by chaos and craziness around us, but this inner sense of self can never be taken away. And the longer we live in the light of the Twelve Steps and actively follow them, the more we develop this strong sense of self.

Today I will stay on the path because it guides me
toward greater development of my self.

When the heart weeps because it has lost, the spirit laughs because it has found.

—Sufi mystic

We must mourn our losses, and for some of us they are many. Whether we lost a loved one, or a marriage, or a job, mourning is a necessary. Mourning is how we acknowledge that what we lost was dear to us and we know it will change us. At the same time, we all know that good things can come from events we never would have chosen. Life does go on and we can grow from our difficulties.

Our clearest example of that is seeing the good that can come from hitting bottom. After our addiction and codependency made us lose all that we could stand to lose, we surrendered to a spiritual program of recovery. Not everyone has to lose so much to gain a vibrant spiritual life. We didn't choose our losses. But for many of us, only after our losses mounted high enough were we opened up to grow spiritually.

Today my spirit laughs because I am alive.

*The name of this infinite and inexhaustible depth and
ground of all being is God. That depth is what the word
God means. And if that word has not much meaning
for you, translate it, and speak to the depths of your
life, of the source of your being, of your ultimate
concern, of what you take seriously without any
reservation.*

—Paul Tillich

In the words of the Twelve Steps, we are guided toward
God, as we understand God. Many of us are at first
turned off by the word *God*. Some of us received early
spiritual guidance through childhood religious training, but others had none at all—and some of us had
negative experiences with organized religion. Now we
are guided to grow into an adult form of spirituality.

The words of today's quotation come from a great
theologian who understood the same wisdom that the
founders of Alcoholics Anonymous did. We don't have
to limit our understanding of God by confining, dog-
matic definitions. Our spiritual life is grounded in
a sense of awe and rises from the deepest part of our
being.

*Today my recovery is restored by God, who surpasses
all understanding.*

*Only your compassion and your loving kindness are
invincible, and without limit.*

—Thich Nhat Hanh

We pray for the wisdom to distinguish between what
we can change and what we cannot. This wisdom re-
sides within our spiritual experience. This spiritual
base is present even when our heart aches at the bed-
side of a loved one whose pain we cannot fix. We can be
at peace in the wisdom of our hearts, knowing that the
best we have to offer is our love and caring. We cannot
do anything that will make a difference in taking away
the pain, but just being there will make an immense
difference.

We know that the spiritual truths that guide our
lives are not based on the concrete world. Yet they light
our paths. We see fear and terror in the world, yet we
can find peace in knowing that our Higher Power will
show us where to walk today. We cannot change the
world today, but we can follow the light provided by
the Twelve Steps. By doing our own small part, we offer
a positive influence.

*Today, as I live in the real world, I will also live in the
spiritual world.*

If a man does his best, what else is there?

—General George S. Patton

Doing our best is not perfection. We have goals and tasks before us. We work at them and we give them our best shot. That is all we need to do, and we deserve to feel all the self-respect any good man feels.

Some of our goals are big challenges. We can set aside any hopes of achieving them perfectly, but when we look back at what we have already done, we may remember that we have come further than we ever dreamed possible. If we expected perfection of ourselves, it would not help us. In fact, it would only get in the way of our work.

Today I give my best to the work that is before me. I will ask nothing more of myself.

I am always doing that which I cannot do, in order that I may learn how to do it.

—Pablo Picasso

We fear trying something that we are not good at. We don't want to do something that we don't already have a handle on. If it isn't our usual way, we doubt that it's right for us. We are afraid of looking foolish, or we are suspicious of things that are unfamiliar.

But let us look at the most accomplished people we know. They didn't achieve greatness by repeating what they already knew. They felt strong enough within themselves—they had the courage—to take risks. Failures were part of their learning and became the basis for greater accomplishment.

Some men get older without ever getting wiser or more grown up. They hold willfully onto what they already know. This lifestyle, living in the light of the Twelve Step program, challenges us to continually push into new territories of growth. We walk on paths where we cannot always see around the next turn. We don't know how to recover before we get on the path of recovery.

Today is another day in which I will do things that push my learning forward.

*The important thing in life is not to have a good hand
but to play it well.*

—Louis N. Fortin

We all admire a man who gets dealt a difficult hand
and plays it well. Most of us have been dealt a mixed
hand in life. We had some bad breaks and some advan-
tages. Many of those things we have no choice about;
our starting point is the situation we find ourselves in.
But we have a lot of choices about how we handle our
situation. We cannot choose to have a lot of wealth
today; we cannot choose to be free of family problems
today; and if we have a health problem, that is what we
must deal with. But we can choose how we will respond to our circumstances, and we can choose what
kind of person we will be.

No one can take away the quality of our character or
the attitude we have toward our situation. We find real
meaning for life when we focus on the choices we can
make. We set our sights on being the best kind of man
we know how to be, even when we have to deal with
tough circumstances.

*Today the meaning I get from life comes from growing
in my strength of character.*

Ritual is the way you carry the presence of the sacred.
Ritual is the spark that must not go out.

—Christina Baldwin

We celebrate birthdays, anniversaries, births, graduations, and holidays. These events mark important times and turning points. Many of us have not honored these rituals, or we have doubted their meaning in life. Some of us have seen rituals used in false and hollow ways, and as a result deprived ourselves of the honest and deep rewards that flow from true and meaningful observances. Many of us are awakening from a time when all of life lost its meaning, and rituals also seemed empty.

Now we are transforming into men who are not cynical, who don't diminish the landmarks in our lives. So we send birthday cards, we light a candle for the memory of a departed grandparent, and we give a gift to acknowledge our partner's special day. The ritual of observing one month of sobriety can be even more meaningful than one decade's observance. All events deserve some attention to mark those times. They bring us to attention. In our humility we accept the attention and we give attention to others.

Today I will take note of important life events and will
plan to mark them with appropriate rituals.

In every marriage more than a week old, there are grounds for divorce. The trick is to find, and continue to find, grounds for marriage.

—Robert Anderson

What is the purpose of a loving partnership? It is to enjoy the relationship. We reach adulthood with only the tools and expectations we learned as children about close relationships. Those childhood experiences, good or bad, are what we unconsciously play out unless we continue to develop. The intensity of adult love and passion can carry us into deep water, beyond our ability to trust, honor, and partner with someone. When we look at what we are asking from our partner, it is often the thing we would ask of the perfect parent.

Now it is time to become adult and carry our share. Rather than focus on what we want in a partner, we need to learn to be the best partner we can be. Each partner sets the standards for a good relationship. We cannot allow ourselves to say, "I only act this way because my partner acts that way." When we don't give that excuse, when we expect the best of ourselves regardless of our partner, we set the standard that we seek, and the relationship changes.

Today I will be the best partner I can be, regardless of what my partner does.

Too often we enjoy the comfort of opinion without the discomfort of thought.

—John F. Kennedy

Recovery from addiction and codependency goes beyond the removal of the substance or the object of our obsession. Stopping our use is the necessary start to recovery. But we can stop using and still continue the thoughts and behavior that set us up for the disease. The biggest downfall for us all is our ego. We have a powerful inner drive to get what we want. To justify our behavior, we may impulsively try to control our surroundings and others. We say that a little bit of the old behavior won't hurt anyone, or we are smarter than others, or our behavior is only for the good of everyone.

We have to be fearless in our self-honesty. And, like dishonesty, honesty builds upon itself: one new self-admission leads to another as we follow this spiritual path. We learn that true humility actually arises from high self-esteem. We learn to rely on our Higher Power to take care of us and guide us. Our development as grown-up men continues for our lifetime.

Today I continue to be more honest with myself than I used to be and continue to behave in healthy ways.

*God is like a mirror. The mirror never changes but
everybody who looks at it sees something different.*

—quoted by Rabbi Harold S. Kushner

In their wisdom, the founders of Alcoholics Anonymous struggled with how to express the spirituality at the core of the program. They landed on the phrase "God *as we understood Him*." That phrase is another way to express the idea of God as a mirror. Even those who try to define God will find that words cannot adequately describe the ultimate creator; instead they place false limits on God.

When we face God, we don't see ourselves as we do in a mirror, but we see beyond ourselves. God provides us with a pathway out of our willful ego-based mind and expands our understanding as participants in the universe of creation. The awe and reverence and meaning of our spiritual lives call us to align ourselves with something far beyond our immediate pleasure and self-satisfying will.

*Today I am grateful for the spiritual awakening that
this program gives me.*

*No one has completed his education who has not
learned to live with an insoluble problem.*

—Edmund J. Kiefer

Facing, for the first time, a stone wall that we cannot
change can be quite a shock. It's a huge emotional
challenge that changes us from boys to men. Some
people first meet their insoluble problem in the form
of the death of a loved one, others through a child
with an incurable handicap, and others by way of a
chronic illness or an addiction. Whatever form a man's
stone wall takes, he naturally responds first with a re-
fusal to accept it and a search for a way around it. But
when he ultimately learns to accept reality, he changes
in a profound way. He has stepped into the world of
adults.

We used to feel that our addiction and codependency were burdens, tragedies that we had to carry. But
there is a bright side to the dark stories of our past:
when we got honest about our powerlessness, we became real men.

*Today I accept my powerlessness once again and feel
grateful for the wisdom it has taught me.*

Better to ask twice than to lose your way twice.

—Danish proverb

How many times have we heard that guys never want to stop and ask for directions? It is true that many of us would rather drive around searching for a place than stop and ask for help. Some of us say we enjoy solving the puzzle without asking for the answer. It's a trait that many men carry to extremes. We apply it to our lives with very serious consequences when we refuse to see a doctor for a medical condition, or we refuse to consult a therapist for personal problems, or we can't bring ourselves to go to a Twelve Step group.

Fortunately we don't have to be permanently locked into those restrictions. We have now found the freedom and rich rewards that come from letting our guard down. The payoff for asking for help, and accepting it, has been far greater than the arrogance of doing everything without help.

Today I will be open to all the help I can get.

*A win in April is just as important as a win in
September.*

—Dave Bristol, major league manager

Hitting bottom and turning to recovery is an important part of our life story. Many of us lost almost everything before we started to recover. Others had the good fortune to get into recovery early, while most parts of our lives were still intact. Some of us relapsed and had to hit bottom more than once. But once we are on the path of recovery, those distinctions make no difference. Nobody is more or less a codependent or an addict. Nobody is immune from the destruction that our old ways would bring if we returned to them.

A high bottom is like a win in April. It doesn't count any less in the long run. It doesn't make us any less an addict or any less codependent, and it doesn't mean that we have any more control than any of our fellow recovering friends. We are all just one bad decision away from reactivating our old ways. The only important distinction is that we are on the path now.

*Today I am grateful to be sober and in recovery,
following this path of a better life.*

The great man is he who does not lose his child-heart.

—Mencius

No matter what we have done or what has happened to us, no matter how guilty, worried, or fearful we feel, there was a time when we were small, innocent, and open-hearted toward the world. That happy and playful boy still lives within us. Sometimes he seems like a distant memory, but we would do well to bring him close to us, give him a place in our awareness, and honor and protect him.

Some of us remembered that little boy being treated too harshly or shamed too deeply, and we adopted false attitudes of disgust toward him. But we can go back still further to a time when he was innocent and we could love him. A strong and healthy man carries that boy close to his heart and lets him come forth to be playful and lighthearted. That boy can be the source of eagerness to learn and hope for the future. He can put himself in the shoes of the small and the weak and treat them with gentleness.

Today my child-heart beats within me as strongly as it ever did.

Marriage is our last best chance to grow up.

—Joseph Barth

Most of us think of marriage in romantic terms. We imagine finding the "right one" and we form a vision of the ideal mate. Others of us have given up on ever finding a lifelong partner. The romance of a relationship naturally plays a less important role as we deal with practical matters like house cleaning, earning a living, and child care. When problems develop, we think about how we want our partner to change. If only they would listen to us more. If only they would spend money more responsibly. If only . . . If only . . .

Most of our ideas about improving our marriage are left over from childhood ideas about how we would like to be taken care of. We want more attention. We want more love. We want to change our partners to satisfy our needs better. But when we give up on changing our partners, we grow up ourselves. When we accept that our partners are also on a life path, which is not identical to our own, we can accept them as friends, and the good things we share grow in importance.

Today I will be a full-grown man, responsible for my part in my intimate relationship, and let the rest go.

*Facing our pain, seeing the enemy as a potential ally,
learning to wait, giving inner events time to ripen
and mature—are methods we can use . . . for
transformation.*

—Harry R. Moody and David Carroll

Sometimes we need to break out of our established
ways of thinking. We need to do what is counterintuitive in order to solve a problem. This program is a
path of personal transformation. We lay the footings
for this transformation by trying something different.
Instead of forcing change, we get out of the way for
change to happen.

We are not being passive and doing nothing. We are
actively engaging in a new way of understanding. Who
or what are my enemies? What am I battling? What if I
look at enemies as potential allies who could teach me
something? What if I didn't work so hard at fixing a
loved one's problems? What if I decide to let a process
evolve and see where it leads?

These transforming ideas create a whole different
set of outcomes. As we try them on, perhaps not only
will the problem be resolved, maybe we ourselves will
be transformed.

*Today I will be open to seeing things in a new way. I
will assume that I don't understand things completely
and I can still learn more.*

Strength and tolerance are partners.

—Kahlil Gibran

We admire strength. As boys we looked up to the raw strength and power we saw in the biceps of big men and older boys. We tested our muscles and those of our pals. We worked at our own physical power to gain the respect of others.

As grown men our admiration has grown up with us. Now we have a much bigger understanding of strength. We know that most strength can't be measured in the size of our muscles. The strongest men are often the kindest and gentlest toward those around them. And often those who are most unsure of their strength try to steal power from others by intimidation, ridicule, and displays of force.

A man stands tallest when he shows tolerance toward those who are different from him and those who are not popular with others. Some say that it builds strength to stand up for others who are vulnerable.

Today I will show tolerance for those who are different or more vulnerable than I am.

To be tested is good. The challenged life may be the best therapist.

—Gail Sheehy

We don't learn anything new from successfully doing things that we have already mastered. We learn from our mistakes and the obstacles that appear in our path. They call on us to come up with new skills. We have certainly come to this path after facing plenty of challenges. And we know that a problem doesn't guarantee that growth will be the outcome.

A problem or a challenge can simply be a net loss until we turn it into an opportunity for growth. If we make a mistake and simply feel stuck in shame and regret, it leads to nothing more. But if we have an element of faith, we can look for its message. That is the path to greater strength and maturity.

Today I will notice my mistakes and use them to grow.

Good thoughts bear good fruit, bad thoughts bear bad fruit—and man is his own gardener.

—James Allen

Before we entered our program of healing and recovery, we didn't recognize our thinking patterns as addictive and codependent. We simply thought our thoughts. Our attitudes seemed natural to us. Now we have learned from looking back that we had many self-serving and distorted ways of seeing life. Because of our need for control and our dependence on addictive ways, we had very nearsighted vision. Many of us indulged in a cynical and dark view of life. We used and controlled others to achieve our needs, and we were often ruled by fear.

Now we are learning that we can cultivate a healthier and happier state of mind. We need not be constantly vigilant about our safety and comfort. We have friends who are genuine and trustworthy. We can rest assured that our Higher Power will always be with us. We are created to be on this earth, and we have a right to take a place among the rest of humankind.

Today I am grateful for a healthy state of mind.

*Experience is not what happens to a man. It is what a
man does with what happens to him.*

—Aldous Huxley

What does it take for a man to be called *experienced*?
Who do we turn to when we look for someone who
knows the ropes? We aren't likely to seek out someone
who has lived a chaotic life and still remains in the
midst of his chaos. But if a man has been there and
learned from his experience, he stands taller than everyone else. He is a kind of hero with much to teach us.

Most of us have plenty of experience. But how can
we learn from our experience? We need to stop, take
time to reflect, and be honest with ourselves. When we
are immersed in busy lives, never taking time to slow
down, we cannot learn from our wealth of experience.
We only pile one event upon another and run from one
demand to another. We can change that by adding
time for reflection and contemplation to our schedule.
A day off with no demands is valuable for the soul. A
retreat to a quiet place, time for fishing, or golf, or hik-
ing is not self-indulgence when we understand that we
are on a spiritual path. Twenty minutes of quiet every
day for solitude and reflection makes us wiser, stronger
men for the lives we are leading.

*Today I will take time to reflect, to be honest with
myself, and to absorb the lessons of my experiences.*

*When I found out I thought God was white, and
a man, I lost interest.*

—Alice Walker

On our path, spiritual development and renewal is
constant. We make time for conscious contact with
God as we understand God, and our understanding
keeps forming. Our childhood images of God may be
too limited. That doesn't mean we have to toss out the
whole concept, but our understanding has to grow up
with us.

To some, God is the spirit and the feeling of camaraderie in group. To some, God is the God expressed in
their traditional religion. Others say that God is simply beyond all definition, an ultimate that exceeds our
rational mind. Others say God is the sense we have
that we are never alone. And to some, God is found in
the beauty of nature. This program of healing and recovery guides us to make a decision to turn our life
and our will over to the God of our understanding.
And we can expect that as the relationship grows so
will our understanding.

*Today I am grateful for the presence of God as I carry
on with my life.*

Storytelling is giving shape to the amorphous chaos
of life.

—Anonymous

When we put words to what has happened to us, we
can begin to learn from our experience. We carry images within us that are the building blocks of our stories, but we only begin to make sense of them when we
put them into words. Talking with a trusted friend, or
speaking in a meeting, or telling a therapist about our
experiences gives them a shape. The words give us a
way to understand, and they build a bridge to others. We may feel deeply alone if we keep our memories
and images to ourselves. When we begin to talk, as we
tell our story, we learn from our own words, and they
take us deeper into our truth.

We don't tell our story only once. We do it over and
over again. It brings relief from the traumas and releases us from the prison of our past. Each time we
talk, even recounting the same events, we are somewhat different because we have grown, and we see our
own story from a new perspective. Listening to other
men's stories and telling our own is one of the special
tools for spiritual growth that we use on this recovery path.

Today I will talk to someone about an experience or
a feeling.

Noble deeds and hot baths are the best cures for depression.

—Dodie Smith

When we change our lives, we give up old patterns. Some of these old patterns, as harmful as they may have been, were like our best friends. We could turn to them for comfort and escape. After giving them up, and after the first elated feelings of liberation, we may also have to deal with the depression and grief of loss.

What should we remember at these times? First of all, depression has a beginning, and it has an end. In the midst of it, we may feel that nothing will ever look good again. That is not so. The loss of energy, the dark mood, the hopelessness—all will pass and we will regain our vitality and joy of life. Second, it helps to stay active. Physical activity is one of the best medicines for a depressed mood: vigorous walks, physical labor, or a good workout at the gym. Another kind of activity is helping others, reaching out to those in need of companionship and a helping hand. It is surprising how good it feels to make a difference in another person's life. The third thing we can do is stop our negative thoughts. We can simply interrupt a train of thought in the same way we might interrupt a conversation and change the subject. Finally, we can take comfort in the faith that our Higher Power will provide what we need in the long run.

Today I will take good care of my mental well-being.

Smooth seas do not make skillful sailors.

—African proverb

Only by meeting many different conditions and being challenged by problems do we develop great skill in dealing with life. We say a man is soft who has always had everything handed to him. We admire a man who has met great challenges and come through them. However, while we are struggling and when the challenges are really on top of us, we may not feel that we are in the midst of some admirable battle. We are more likely to simply feel burdened and stressed, not knowing what the outcome will be.

When the sailor is in the midst of the storm, he focuses intently upon what he has to do right now. He learns to read the wind and the waves in these extreme conditions by being there and by learning from others who are more experienced. That is a model for developing our skills on this sea of life.

Today I will focus on what I need to do just for today, and I will learn from those who are more experienced than I am.

The wise person questions himself, the fool others.

—Henri Arnold

We pray for wisdom and sometimes we achieve it. The strongest and wisest of men are not threatened by questioning their own answers. If we draw conclusions and blindly stick to them, we can never learn anything new. We have often made the mistake of avoiding the appearance of ignorance. Instead, we are at our best when we give ourselves the privilege of being a learner.

When someone tells us something we don't understand or agree with, our best response is to ask for more information. We can take our ego out of the equation, surrender our need to be right, and simply try to learn what is being told to us. What is it that I don't understand here? What does the other person see that I am missing? When we attain a moment of wisdom, we are open to learning.

Today I will give myself the privilege of being a learner.

The creative process is a process of surrender,
not control.

—Julia Cameron

When creative artists describe the experience of creating a painting or writing a novel, they often talk about feeling that they are given inspiration, as if it comes from outside them. They tell us that if they are too willful or too deliberate, they get in the way.

When we begin to walk the Twelve Steps, we enter that same kind of process. We are led to surrender—not in defeat, but to let ourselves be cared for. As men we may know little about becoming so vulnerable. Many of us concluded long ago that vulnerability only led to pain and defeat. Perhaps we could let a lover care for us, especially in an erotic or sexual way. But opening ourselves to the care of our group, our sponsor, our Higher Power was outside anything we had ever tried.

On this path, our whole life is a creative process. We can't know exactly where it will take us. That is the adventure—and it is infinitely long. We continue the creative way, daily learning new things and developing new experiences. We are present and open, and we know the feeling of being spiritually awake.

Today my life will be a creative adventure.

*God provides minimum protection, maximum
support.*

—William Sloane Coffin

People often ask how a just God could allow innocent
children to starve to death, or how an all-powerful God
could send devastating storms that cause pain and destruction across the land. Great theologians tell us that
we cannot hold God responsible for the evil and pain in
the world. Bad things happen, and they aren't the work
of God. In a random universe, God's design is to be
present with us and support us through the troubles
we face.

When we turn our life and will over to the care of
God, we can't expect God to bring us special magical
favors. Instead we turn over our willfulness and childish demanding nature to God who helps us be strong,
maintain our spirit, and continue on our path. Then
God never leaves us alone, even when we defy God,
even when we make bad choices. God is there loving
us, even when we feel worthless.

*Today I will open myself to the support of my
Higher Power.*

It's just human. We all have the jungle inside us. We all have wants and needs and desires, strange as they may seem.

—Diane Frovlov and Andrew Schneider,
Northern Exposure

Sex is a driving force in our lives. Many of us in recovery find that our sexuality is another part of our lives that is changing. Some of us suddenly find we can't perform in sobriety as we did while we were using. Others of us are recovering from addiction to sexual behaviors. When we are facing difficulty with our sexuality, it is sometimes hard to think of it as a source of pleasure and reward.

In fact our sexuality can recover and heal, just as any other aspect of our personality can recover. Grown-up, adult sex is more comfortable, more sensuous, and more fulfilling than adolescent sex. That is only possible when we are sober and awake to our lives. Many of us need to start by tuning in to our bodies and the sensations we experience now in our sobriety. Along with that, we may need to embrace the fact that we deserve to have sexual pleasure, not as something we are owed, but as something we can seek and indulge in. These changes happen gradually over time as recovery progresses.

Today I am grateful for the energizing force of sex and passion in my life.

Solitude is the furnace of transformation.

—Henri Nouwen

In solitude we quietly unwrap the honesty that is deep within us. Sitting in the company of just ourselves and God, we gradually realize that no one else is observing us and the image we present. Solitude may throw us into some confusion at first, or some discomfort. We might feel pushed to escape, to get out of there into a place with some action and distractions. Transformation is frightening because it is a process that we do not fully control. We can block it, or stop it, but if we allow it to progress, it is controlled by our deeper honesty and by the spirit of a Higher Power.

We can make a simple decision that we will enter the experience of solitude. We can do that for a few minutes every day in a special place we set aside, or we can set aside several days of retreat. However, we cannot create our own transformation by a simple decision. Our solitude prepares us and softens the guards we have set against the frightening process of transformation. And as we are ready, change and growth arrives.

Today I will open myself through moments of solitude.

September

□ □ □ □ □ □ □

*I have a great deal more respect for someone who keeps
coming back after losing heartbreaker after heartbreaker than I do for the winner who has everything
going for him.*

—Wilt Chamberlain

One aspect of recovery is dealing with relapse. After we
have been in recovery and then fall back into our addiction or codependent behaviors, we are filled with regret. We may also be stricken with strong feelings of
shame and a defeatist attitude. But if we come back to
our meetings and get back on the program, we deserve
only self-respect. We are not defeated unless we give up
on ourselves.

No bad experience is a total loss unless we refuse to
learn something from it. Recovery from relapse begins
when we relearn that we are powerless over our addiction. It calls for us to make something positive out of
the negative experience. We examine the point where
we resumed our addictive and codependent thinking,
even before we realized it. Experienced people in the
program know that we learn to prevent relapse by returning to recovery after we have fallen away.

*Today I have the greatest respect for those who keep
coming back.*

It is with our passions as with fire and water: they make good servants but bad masters.

—Aesop

Our passions—whether they be sex, anger, love, or an intense interest in a hobby—are energizing and enriching dimensions of our lives. On the other hand, who hasn't made mistakes with his passions? Who hasn't had regrets about his actions when a drive became a master rather than a servant? Some of us are recovering from problems with anger or sex. Many of us are subject, in our recovery, to overinvolvement with some new passion, such as work or a hobby, that once again takes us away from our relationships and our peace of mind.

A man grows up by making mistakes and learning from them. We learn to steer a car by turning the wheel, overcorrecting, and recorrecting. It is when we refuse to acknowledge that our passion has become our master that we cannot make the needed adjustments to keep our passions in balance. Keeping an honest, unflinching personal inventory is what a strong man does.

Today I am grateful for the passions that serve my well-being.

Our faith should quell our fears, never our courage.

—William Sloane Coffin

Courage is a core value for a man, but without fear, there is no need for courage. Our path to this point in our lives was governed by fear more than most of us ever realized or wanted to admit. We were driven into the arms of addiction and codependency by fear and anxiety. Our substance of choice gave us a feeling of control, and we developed a knee-jerk habit of grasping for it. Even before our fears for our well-being could rise to consciousness, we were scanning the world for ways to gain that sense of control. For some of us that meant anxiously controlling the people around us; for others it meant running off to the casino or escaping into pornography.

The centerpiece of our recovery is a completely different way to soothe our uneasiness. It is a belief that if we turn to a Higher Power, we can quell our fears and find serenity without the destructiveness of our old habits. We learned the old ways over time and this new way takes time to learn as well. We can start immediately to turn our life over to a Higher Power and as we do, we will find greater comfort in return.

Today I will admit my fears and anxieties, finding courage by turning to faith in a Higher Power.

If people concentrated on the really important things in life, there'd be a shortage of fishing poles.

—Doug Larson

We win admiration for work, achievement, and competitiveness. We are told that a good man is a good provider. These are external rewards, but the rewards of relaxing, of rest and quiet solitude, of recreation are not external. We feel those rewards internally. They are the rewards of personal growth. Work addiction is a tempting mistake for us recovering men. We had big problems in the past and it feels wonderful to know that we can be competent in our work. We lived in crisis and our lives were out of control; that memory can haunt us for a lifetime, so work may now provide a welcome structure. But too much work can be another distraction from the important things.

Sometimes we may need to schedule some free time with our families and with our friends, time simply for loafing. Taking a half hour each day for quiet thought and reflection, with no external sign of accomplishment, helps us to become better men.

Today I will lighten my focus on work and make time for play.

Nothing happens unless first a dream.

—Carl Sandburg

Knowing ourselves is partly a matter of forming our dreams for who we want to become. These dreams are constantly evolving as long as we live. They give us purpose in our daily lives and point us in the direction we want to go. We can advance our growth by taking pencil and paper and quickly jotting down our dreams and goals. This simple list can be carried in our billfold, and we can react to it and modify it over time.

Sometimes we resist writing these things down, or even thinking about them, because we may not dare to admit our true motivations and dreams. But even if we don't admit our dreams, they still shape our behavior. When we acknowledge what we most want, we become better men.

Today I will take the risk to form a clear idea of my fondest dreams.

Never bear more than one kind of trouble at a time. Some people bear all three—all they have had, all they have now, and all they expect to have.

—Edward Everett Hale

Learning to manage our worries and our darker memories is part of becoming a stronger person. If we don't exercise some choice over them, we can get swallowed up in a chain reaction: one problem ignites fear and pain about all the others. Understanding the wisdom of powerlessness becomes an excellent guide for us in focusing our mind when troubles assail us.

We accept that many things aren't within our control to create or to stop. All we can do is hope and pray and turn the results over to our Higher Power. We don't subject ourselves to a pity session or a major anxiety attack by letting one challenge remind us of everything that has gone wrong in the past or could go wrong tomorrow. We live in the present, we deal with what is before us at the moment, and we pray for the serenity to accept the rest.

Today I will live in the present.

*You never really understand a person until you
consider things from his point of view.*

—Harper Lee

We came to this spiritual path with habits and addictions that had trapped us in a very childish and self-centered mind. Our strong need for control, our sense that we could count only on ourselves blocked us from learning to understand others. Now we are finding a fellowship in which we don't have to be alone. Others reach out to us in helpful and generous ways. We have friends.

The wonderful thing about a good friend is that we gain the opportunity to see through someone else's eyes. We can borrow this person's life experiences as if they were our own and learn those lessons without making the same mistakes. Or we can borrow our friend's feeling of hope when our own hope is flagging. It's not necessary to agree with someone to see things from his point of view. Sometimes we simply enlarge our scope by saying, "I see why you could feel that way." The fellowship of good friends is one of the most humanizing experiences we can have.

*Today I will listen to others and try to borrow their
eyes and ears.*

Learn the alchemy true human beings know: The
moment you accept what troubles you've been given,
the door will open.

—Rumi

Step One requires us to admit the trouble we face. We now know that until we do that, no progress can be made. Some of us honestly didn't see the true nature of our powerlessness. Others knew the truth but refused to admit it. Once we have faced up to such a big admission of powerlessness, we start to see an important pattern. Now we can apply it to many everyday situations. Owning up to the truth of a problem opens the door. Something changes and we begin to deal with problems in a new and more effective way.

Whether we have diabetes that needs daily attention, or a child with special needs, or a work situation that never improves, the formula is the same. Accept the matter for what it is, as hard as that may be, and new answers begin to emerge. In part, this is a spiritual process that seems to naturally lead us to the next step of turning to our Higher Power for comfort and guidance. This readies us for new possibilities.

Today I will try to accept the reality that I face so that
I am ready for new answers.

Anyone who keeps the ability to see beauty never grows old.

—Franz Kafka

We ask ourselves, what really counts when everything else is stripped away? What do we still value? Beauty is one of those values for many of us. It might be the beauty of the outdoors, solitude in the wilderness, a symphony, a special painting, or the athletic grace of a pitcher as he hurls the baseball across home plate. Something stirs within us when we see beauty. Many would call that a spiritual experience because it seems to touch the soul of our being.

We can feel vulnerable when we have such experiences, and some of us have learned to run roughshod over those moments. We smother that part of our soul so that we don't have to feel our manhood threatened. Now we are learning new lessons. We are growing into stronger, more open, and more spiritual men. Beauty, wherever we see it, is part of our spiritual life.

Today I am open to the stirring in my soul when I see beauty.

*There are no secrets to success. It is the result of
preparation, hard work, learning from failure.*

—Colin Powell

Preparation consists of becoming entirely ready. On
this path, where we have faced the ultimate truth of
powerlessness, we accept the deep wisdom of adulthood: some things cannot be changed by the force of
our will. So our work is to make ourselves ready for
change to come to us. We work on our willfulness, our
moral character, our honesty, and our openness to the
spiritual presence. Readiness means that when opportunities for change appear, we accept them. It means
that change comes as a gift, not of our own invention.

As our relationship with ourself grows, our relationships with others improve. As our relationship with
our Higher Power grows, the cravings that we could not
subdue by force of will are simply and quietly lifted. It
is a spiritual paradox: this is not a passive path we are
walking; it requires hard work. And yet the success we
find is a gift that comes to us and we can only accept it.

*Today I will continue to work, making myself ever
more ready to receive the gifts of the spirit.*

I don't have to be what you want me to be.

—Muhammad Ali

We only truly become ourselves from the inside out. During our active addiction many of us tried so hard to please others that we lost any sense of who we were, or we created an external image that would get others to like us. Some of us lost ourselves in codependently taking care of others. So much focus on others never led us to know ourselves or truly develop our interior private self.

This program, with its twelve suggested Steps, is really a road map for the formation of a true self. At the beginning we may feel empty inside, as if hardly any self exists. But at least some small, undeveloped self is always there, and it will grow. By taking inventory of ourselves, by becoming accountable for our actions, and by developing our spirituality, we become truly whole.

Today I will be the person I know from inside myself and not try to create an image to please others.

*Abuse is something that is done to us. It is not who
we are.*

—Euan Bear and Peter Dimock

Everyone has some experience with being treated
badly. Sometimes that experience leaves us with scars
that affect us for years. Abuse is the feeling of being
overwhelmed by someone's power to hurt us or use us.
It steals our basic human dignity. Afterward we feel belittled, as if something basic about us is missing or
blemished.

Recovery means we restore our feeling of personal
dignity. To begin that part of our recovery, we first
name the abuse. Someone beat us up, someone called
us names, or someone used our body for his or her
own pleasures. Abuse may even come from someone
we love and trust. After we name the abuse, we tell a
trusted friend what happened. In this process we start
the work of placing those experiences outside of ourselves instead of holding them deep inside where they
confuse us. Ultimately, our recovery frees us.

*Today I understand that even though bad things
happened to me, I am basically good, just like everyone else.*

You can learn little from victory. You can learn
everything from defeat.

—Christy Mathewson

We all know the face of painful defeat. We tried to win,
but some of our ways led to disgrace and shame. We
used unwise and self-indulgent methods to cope with
life's problems. Those defeats were devastating. But it's
not only bad choices and mistakes that create loss and
heartache. Inevitably, adult life forces everyone to face
powerlessness. That is a spiritual lesson that some of
us accept more readily than others. Many guys don't
easily give up the heady feeling of power and the pride
of doing things their own way, even when their own
way brings repeated defeat.

With only victories, we might remain as superficial
boys for the rest of our lives. What would push us to
learn? From the broken pieces of painful events we are
forced to learn something new. We can no longer hold
on to our voracious appetites and our stubborn willfulness. We have to finally open our minds to the wisdom
of others. Through our failures we are strengthened. In
facing powerlessness, we truly grow from boyishness
into genuine manhood.

Today I am grateful for all that I have learned from
my defeats.

I began to have an idea of my life, not as the slow shaping of achievement to fit my preconceived purposes, but as the gradual discovery and growth of a purpose which I did not know.

—Joanna Field

When we pledge to turn our life and our will over to the care of God, we have taken a profound step. With those words we enter into the mystery of the spiritual life. We move from feeling alone to trusting that our Higher Power will guide our choices. We move from focusing on what we want to focusing on who we will become. We stop trying to control everything and become open to the mystery that underlies life.

For some of us, today presents challenges and worries. Some of us are anxious about a problem at work or within our family. We may have a painful dispute with our life partner. In the wisdom of the spiritual path, we can lean back on the faith that we don't have to deal with these things alone. We can do what is possible, and we can rely on the care of God to work in the ways of God.

Today I am grateful for the care and purposes of God to lead me in dealing with life.

It's not true that nice guys finish last. Nice guys are winners before the game even starts.

—Addison Walker

Being considerate, civil, generous, and interested in others forms the basis of good character and good relationships with others. When we stop being so focused on ourselves, when we stop trying to come out ahead of everyone else, our world opens up. We suddenly have good, supportive friendships that are more valuable than material winnings.

The Golden Rule is ancient advice that is expressed in many languages and world religions. It says, "Do unto others as you would have them do unto you." It is a small man who takes away someone else's power to advance his own. A strong man can confidently cheer for the strength of others.

Today I am grateful for the good friends in my life.

If stupidity got us into this mess, then why can't it get us out?

—Will Rogers

When we are in the midst of our worst problems, we often behave stubbornly, trying harder to gain control of what is out of control. Because we feel alone, or because we insist on doing things our own way, we repeatedly apply the same solutions that repeatedly produce the same problems. We forget that as human beings we require the help of others to live happy and healthy lives. We need all the help we can get. Without the input and wisdom of others, we are stuck with our limited or mistaken ideas.

Perhaps today we are faced with problems that have no clear solutions. We can't see an obvious way around them, and we can't see a new answer. The sooner we accept our true nature and bring others into our questions, the sooner we will be able to consider new ideas and take in the wisdom of our friends.

Today I resolve to talk to my friends about the matters that weigh on my mind.

If a man does his best, what else is there?

—General George S. Patton

For many of us, competition is so ingrained that we have a knee-jerk competitive reaction to almost every encounter with another man. Competition is great fun among friends. Testing our skill, our power, and our wits against others helps us know ourselves better and shows us what we are capable of. It is a kind of closeness among friends to playfully compete. But when competition becomes our only way to relate to others, it keeps people away. When we can only respond with a wisecrack or a one-up comment, we are just a one-trick pony, reacting out of weakness and fear of getting close.

Among true and trusted friends, a man is entitled to show more than his strength and his guarded side. A true friend doesn't use our vulnerability or our mistakes to take advantage of us. When he holds them as a trust that he guards and protects, he shows the mark of true friendship.

Today I will be the best person that I can be, and that includes honesty about my weaknesses and vulnerability.

*There is no saint without a past—no sinner without
a future.*

—Shri Haidakhan Babaji

How can we not believe in redemption when we see it
demonstrated all around the room every time we attend a meeting? Our most respected members were
once in crisis at the bottom of their lives. And when we
contemplate our own feelings of guilt and shame, we
need humility to accept the fact that we, too, can be restored. All saints and all sinners reflect the same truth:
all human beings are imperfect. If we are truly humble,
we can accept our humanity, stop expecting perfection,
and forgive our mistakes.

We take our personal inventory and assume responsibility for our actions because that process starts to
release us from guilt and shame. The most dignified
man is not the guy who never made a mistake, but the
one who faced his mistakes and went forward living a
better life.

*Today I am grateful for the redemption this program
leads me toward.*

Man must search for what is right, and let happiness
come on its own.

—Johann Pestalozzi

We make a mistake when we try to pursue happiness as
if it were something we could achieve and hold. Happiness comes and goes. It is a by-product. If we seek to
become better men, to fulfill our deeper values, happiness will visit us along the way. On the other hand, to
seek happiness as a goal and expect to hold on to it will
only bring frustration and self-pity.

Our human nature calls us to have goals and values
that transcend the limits of our own selves. We feel
deep love for our children and we want to be the best
father possible. When we fulfill that goal, we feel happy.
We have a great love for music or art, and we want to
participate in it by creating it or appreciating it. When
we fulfill that desire, we feel happy. Hard work is not
often thought of as happiness, but its outcome often
brings happiness.

Today I am working for goals that I believe in.
Happiness will come and go along the way.

Prayer is not asking. It is a longing of the soul. It is daily admission of one's weakness.

—Mahatma Gandhi

We got into our difficulties because of the ways we managed our desires and longings. When we found ways to easily cool our pain or satisfy our longings, we got hooked on them. After we learned that our controlling and addictive behaviors could make us feel comfortable and bring intense pleasure, we got even more hooked on them. But they quickly proved to be false answers.

Now we are a bit wiser, and we strive to avoid those alluring pitfalls. So we daily turn in prayer to our Higher Power. This is the longer, slower approach to managing our desires and longings. Ultimately what we sought in the easy answers was something deeper, more satisfying. Through our spiritual life we find satisfaction to our longings and yearnings.

Today I bring my powerlessness to a Higher Power for care and guidance.

For man, autumn is a time of harvest, of gathering together. For nature, it is a time of sowing, of scattering abroad.

—Edwin Way Teale

Autumn is a good metaphor for the Twelfth Step. In this Step we are reaping the benefits of recovery, but it is also important for continued recovery that we spread the word. It is a time to tell our stories and invite others to have what we have found. Nature sustains itself not by hoarding and keeping its bounty locked up, but by generously and prolifically scattering its seeds to the wind. We need to do the same in recovery.

The early recoverers who discovered the path that became the Twelve Steps quickly recognized that their own precarious progress required them to tell their stories to other alcoholics. They asked permission from other suffering addicts to be allowed to tell their stories, not to promote their method, but to sustain their own progress. We, too, need to tell other people where we have been and what we have found.

Today I will be generous in giving away what I have learned.

Never give in. Never give in. Never, never, never, never, never—in nothing, great or small, large or petty—never give in.

—Winston Churchill

In the Serenity Prayer we seek to accept the things we cannot change and to change the things we can. Many of us have been discouraged by repeated relapses and by overwhelming problems. This is a time when we need to discern between what we can and cannot change. A man with diabetes, after first losing his eyesight and then one leg to his disease, says that he carries on, loving life, because he still chooses to have purpose and meaning. He cannot change his disease; he has to accept it.

Our heroes aren't the guys who had it easy. The greatest heroes are always the ones who battled with discouragement and great challenges. A relapse isn't the end of the story. We have risked losing everything, including our lives, but if we survived, we never go back to square one. Our past, no matter how dark, is a resource to build upon. If we have relapsed, we don't lose what we learned in our past time of recovery. We only need to diligently learn from our mistakes and return to what we know recovery still offers.

Today I resolve to never give up on life.

> *To be sensual is to respect and rejoice in the force of life itself, and to be present in all that one does, from the effort of loving to the breaking of bread.*
>
> —Phyl Garland

Sensuality and sexuality are very spiritual experiences. When we take pleasure in our senses and take joy in life, we reach into the spiritual realm. We enter that realm when we are present in the moment, drinking in the warmth of the bright sunshine, smelling the freshness of the air, savoring the aroma of toast in the morning, relishing good music, or indulging in the good feelings of touch and gentle eye contact.

Of course this sensual side can be distorted. Many of us have been so taken with sensuality that we got lost in it. We corrupted our spirituality with bad judgment or abusive behaviors. Now we are growing into good men who love life and respect the wonders of sex and sensuality. We are learning to be present to all sensations, to the very force of life as we experience it, and as adults we are wisely choosing when to indulge in them heartily.

Today I celebrate all my senses and seek a happy, healthy sexuality.

> *The remarkable thing is that we really love our neighbor as ourselves: we do unto others as we do unto ourselves. We hate others when we hate ourselves. We are tolerant toward others when we tolerate ourselves. We forgive others when we forgive ourselves. We are prone to sacrifice others when we are ready to sacrifice ourselves.*

—Eric Hoffer

Our healing begins within ourselves. We may have deep feelings of low self-esteem. We didn't grow up believing that we were good. We may carry feelings of guilt for bad choices we made. We may not expect to be loved, and when the love is there, we may not see it for what it is.

That is where we must start our recovery. We must treat ourselves with respect, forgive our wrongs, and accept forgiveness. A good man with strong self-esteem doesn't think he is without fault or superior to others. He knows that he is a mixture of many qualities, good and bad, as all people are. He doesn't attack his own nature by calling himself stupid. When we learn to treat ourselves with the respect that our creator has for us, our love and respect are reflected in all of our relationships.

Today I pledge to be respectful and forgiving toward myself.

*No one can begin to feel better about oneself until
brutal self-honesty prevails.*

—Donna Thompson

We have sometimes used words to fool ourselves
and fool others. We say "I'll try" when we really don't
want to face a challenge. Or we say "I'll think about
that" when we simply want to avoid talking about
something.

Some challenges in life require action. Nothing less
will do. Do we say that we will "try" to call our sponsor,
or do we call him? Do we "try" to work on a Step for
our recovery, or do we work on it? When someone gives
us a word of wisdom that we don't want to hear, do we
engage with him, perhaps even tell him it's hard for us
to hear, or do we say "I'll think about that" just to get
him off our back?

*Today I will not fool myself. I will use words that admit
my truth.*

The Lord created me at the beginning of his work,
The first of his acts of long ago.

—Proverbs 8:22

All of God's creation deserves respect. Many of us have felt that we were bad or worthless, or beyond the reach of genuine acceptance. If we believed in God, perhaps we thought we deserved God's condemnation more than we deserved grace. Today we are reminded that we are part of creation. God is everywhere in creation and within us.

Certainly some of our actions were wrong. Certainly we must be accountable for our bad deeds. But what we do is not who we are. Our deeds are not our spirit. At the core, we are sacred creatures of God. Being accountable is a high and noble thing, and it is one way that we pay respect to ourselves and our God.

Today I will respect myself as part of God's work.

The heart forms itself according to what it loves.

—Theresa Gerhardinger

All great spiritual traditions speak to us about our desires and how we manage them. Their universal wisdom tells us that our handling of our yearnings and attachments affects the kind of person we become. For us addicts and codependents this has special meaning. We may have fallen in love with alcohol, or a drug, or another behavior. As codependents, we also become so committed to the care and control of others that we never develop our own spirit. One man said that alcoholism, at its core, is man's search for God. Of course, that answer is a false hope that leads to death, not life.

The Twelve Steps sprang up as a practical path showing the way to face up to our desires and not be ruled by them. It isn't easy, but it's a challenge with human proportions. It's not something we do once and have it over with. Our lives and our hearts are shaped on a daily basis over time by what we choose to love.

Today I am grateful for my freedom to love the people and the things that give life.

Never look down to test the ground before taking the next step; only he who keeps his eyes fixed on the far horizon will find his right road.

—Dag Hammarskjöld

When we first learned to drive, we had to develop the skill of fixing our eyes far down the highway rather than immediately in front of the car. In our lives, we also need the bigger picture. When we were caught in our pursuit of immediate gratification and crisis management, we didn't have time to look at where it was all leading.

Now we have a better idea of what our bigger goals are. Larger values guide our choices; we no longer focus only on immediate relief or satisfying today's appetites. Naming our goals and our deepest values gives us the guidance to steer our course smoothly and become the kind of man we want to be.

Today I will name goals and values, and they will guide me.

Not until we are lost do we begin to understand ourselves.

—Henry David Thoreau

Growth and development never happens in a straight line. Events may surprise and challenge us. A man thinks he is on a path to success and suddenly loses his job. A student takes a challenging class and fails an important test. A professional truck driver is involved in a serious accident. These events that fall into our lives are horrible things to deal with. Yet we have to respond to them. They show us the edge of what we know and force us to push further.

It is always the lost feeling that opens us up to grow and learn. When we are lost, it is in finding ourselves again that we grow deeper.

Today I accept the challenges I face because I have no other option, and I will use them to shape my growth in a positive direction.

Chains do not hold a marriage together. It is threads,
hundreds of tiny threads, which sew people together
through the years.

—Simone Signoret

A relationship may begin with love at first sight. Some
of us have experienced that feeling many times. But
the growth of a relationship is nutured by sharing
many experiences and times together. We live through
many kinds of events, including the unexpected turns
that every life brings. We have enjoyable times together,
and we inevitably disappoint each other or frustrate
each other. The history we build over time is the store-
house of our lives.

Sometimes when a relationship is strained, we easily
say to ourselves, *I could do better without this; I could find*
someone else and have a better life. But to walk away from
a relationship would be to walk away from a shared
history. Some relationships are so toxic that it is better
to cut our losses and leave. But usually we are happier
when we can repair the wrongs and build upon our
history.

Today I am grateful for the history I share with my
intimate partner.

October

I can't stand it when a player whines to me or his teammates or his wife or the writers or anyone else. A whiner is almost always wrong. A winner never whines.

—Paul Brown

Sometimes when we get lost in our complaints about our lot in life, it is just a way of staying stuck. We spin out woeful thoughts about why our life is so difficult. This is just another way of being self-centered. When we are lost in that jungle, we may need someone else to alert us to what we are doing.

Everyone has difficult circumstances. No one gets to choose all the circumstances he faces. Many challenges in life are of our own making, but many others are just random events. The way out of self-pity is to remember that we are just like everyone else. And we, like the whole human race, have the job of making our way through the wilderness of our life. Exactly what we accomplish is less important than what kind of man we are as we do it.

Today I accept my life and continue to move ahead and grow as a person.

Not everything that can be counted counts, and not everything that counts can be counted.

—Albert Einstein

In following the healing way, we open ourselves to truths that can never be established as concrete facts. Some of us have always been comfortable with a spiritual outlook. But some of us were hurt by damaging or even abusive experiences in religious institutions and gave up on them as meaningless. Now we all come together on a path that takes a very wide view of spirituality while making spiritual ideas central.

It is reassuring to learn that one of the greatest scientists of all time had a firm respect for realities that could not be pointed to or quantified. He excelled in the practical, objective world of science and he also knew about spiritual truth. Now we, too, are learning how our spiritual life creates miracles we could not bring about by the force of our will.

Today I am grateful to be tuned in to those forces that are outside objective, concrete reality.

Be grateful for luck. Pay the thunder no mind—listen to the birds. And don't hate nobody.

—Eubie Blake

Some mornings we wake and the bright sun warms our bodies and our spirits. Other mornings we wake to darkness and feel a heavy shroud of worry surrounding us. In order to be present for life, a man needs to carry the big picture of life's cycles in his mind. Small children don't have the big picture. They haven't yet experienced the ups and downs of daily life. But our adult life has taught us that the bad times pass and the bright sun returns.

A strong man doesn't deny the darkness, but he learns to cope with it by choosing what he pays attention to. There may be thunder, but we listen for the birdsong. We don't lose our gratitude for the good luck we have had so far and for the constant companionship of our Higher Power. We care for our relationships and they sustain us through the darkest times.

Today I accept the cycles of life and I am grateful for the good fortune that has carried me this far.

*The more we allow ourselves to be servants of having,
the more we shall let ourselves fall prey to the gnawing
anxiety which having involves.*

—Gabriel Marcel

In our consumer-driven world we are flooded with
tempting advertising images that promise us happiness, power, and virility if we buy these products. Success in this consumer world means financial wealth
rather than good character or playing the hand we
are dealt. The phrase *quality of life* often refers to material wealth, not to the quality of one's personal
relationships.

We are following an alternative path. On this path,
material goods are just trappings to be used and
shared, never to define us. Our worth as a man is never
measured by the car we drive or the clothes we wear.
The guy who drives an old beater and the guy in a hot
sports car are equals. No matter how many toys we
have, and no matter how badly we have screwed up our
lives, God loves His creation and wants the best for us.

*Today I will keep my eye on the real ingredients of my
"quality of life."*

*Despite all the obvious distinctions between men and
women, our hearts share the same fears and yearnings.
Learning how to hold each other's hearts tenderly is the
art of love making.*

—David Treadway

Intimacy is showing our inner self to another person.
When we live in an intimate partnership, our task is to
learn to be worthy of the trust and vulnerability our
partner opens to us. At the same time, we need to learn
to show our fears and yearnings to our beloved. When
we make disrespectful, sarcastic, or hurtful comments,
we show ourselves as unworthy of the intimate vulnerability our partner granted to us. When we are open and
intimate with our partner, we deserve to be treated
with tenderness and respect.

This kind of intimacy is not easy to achieve or maintain. It is a very grown-up kind of relationship that we
learn to achieve as adults.

*Today I will be vulnerable with my partner and honor
my partner's trust in me.*

The other planets may not be able to support life, but it isn't easy on this one either.

　　　　　　　　　　　　　　　　—Anonymous

The difficulties and pleasures of life always seem to come as a mixture of both. Today's hard problems will be different by tomorrow. And the pleasures and rewards that come our way always come in waves of greater and lesser measure. That perspective on life's problems is what we need to continue on our path of personal growth. Today we no longer reach for the instant relief of a drug or a behavior to get an immediate good feeling.

In the midst of all the trees, we look up and see the bigger picture of the forest. The problems at hand today will pass. Our task is to examine the problem, then decide what we can do about it and what we can simply turn over to our Higher Power. By keeping our perspective on the bigger picture, we will not get lost in the anxiety of the present moment.

Today I am grateful that I can count on my Higher Power for help in dealing with my difficulties.

*Never does the human soul appear so strong and
noble as when it forgoes revenge and dares to forgive
an injury.*

—E. H. Chapin

Forgiveness is a spiritual process. Little children always
justify their hitting and aggressive behavior by claiming "He started it!" Throughout life, we all have justifi-
cations for our resentments. We all feel hurt by others
at times. Our spiritual journey asks us to face these af-
fronts with a more grown-up mind than we had as
small boys. Our immature and undisciplined ego may
play a role in how we respond to an offense today.

Much of the time, when we are hurt, another's actions are not really about us. They are a reflection on
the person who did them, not on us. We are not in the
center of that picture, and if we take our overgrown ego
out of it, we can see that. Sometimes we have to defend
ourselves, but we don't have to hold on to the resentments. Only after we have grown strong enough can we
see that our most dignified response is to let the inci-
dent be about the other person, and finally forgive
that person.

*Today I will take my ego out of the picture, let others'
actions reflect on them, and strive to forgive them.*

Forgiveness ought to be like a canceled note, torn in two and burned up, so that it can never be shown against the man.

—Henry Ward Beecher

When we have been hurt or offended, we naturally have strong feelings about it. Sometimes we want to leap to forgiveness as a cover for our wounds because we fear the damage to the relationship. In that case forgiveness comes too soon, before we even let ourselves know what we feel. More often, our ego has been bruised and, primitively, it wants revenge. But it is we who carry those angry feelings and nurse our negative inner world. And it is we who must find a way to live in a more positive state of mind.

Some of our angers and resentments may be decades old. No repayment can ever settle the account. Maybe we didn't get what we needed from our parents, or a former spouse treated us badly, or a co-worker or boss was unnecessarily harsh. We can lighten our burden by simply tearing up the unpaid debt. In a spiritual sense, we can leave the other guy's conscience to him and his maker. By declaring old debts forgiven, we are free to live in the present as happier, better men.

Today I will strive to let go of old resentments so I can live more fully in the present.

You don't have to suffer to be a poet; adolescence is enough suffering for anyone.

—John Ciardi

We can think of our life as a poem. We are crafting a meaningful whole out of chaotic experiences. How do we make something worthwhile from what our life has been? We begin by getting honest with ourselves and others. We all have had enough suffering to feel deeply. We all have come face to face with the stone wall of facts we cannot change by our own efforts.

The ultimate creation of a man's life is in who he becomes. We have lost a lot. We have had sufficient pain, and we are guilty of doing bad things. Now we take that bundle of experiences and ask, what can I learn from them? All that we have done can be turned into something heroic and wonderful. There is nothing more inspiring than a mess of a man who works hard and turns himself into a good person.

Today I will continue my path to creating a life with meaning and quality.

In America, sex is an obsession; in other parts of the world it is a fact.

—Marlene Dietrich

Most of us were given conflicting lessons about sex, and we were often confused about how to fulfill our sexual nature. As young boys, some of us were told that our sexual impulses were bad. At the same time, we were told that sex is a sacred gift from God. Many of us grew up to have regrets about our sexual activities. Some of us were captured by pornography, turning others into sex objects. And sex became a drug of escape for many of us.

Our spiritual goal is to fulfill our sexual and erotic nature in joyful, safe, and respectful ways. We move past our sexual anxieties by accepting the fact that sexual pleasure is God-given. It is simply a fact of life and its value depends upon how it is used. It is neither the path to life fulfillment nor the devil's creation. When we align our sexuality with the rest of our lives, it is a pathway to connection and intimacy.

Today I am grateful for my sexual nature and will express it in ways that I respect.

*Love consists in this, that two solitudes protect and
touch and greet each other.*

—Rainer Maria Rilke

Mature love is a powerful and wonderful thing that
has to be learned in adulthood. Children are certainly
capable of loving and receiving love, but they are not
yet fully formed as individuals. Adult intimacy is like a
bridge spanning the space between two people. When
our intimate partner confides in us and becomes vulnerable, our task is to make that moment safe. And
when we become vulnerable, we have a right to the
same safety—which means no disrespect and no de-
meaning or abusive behavior. When someone puts
trust in us, it is our duty to honor it.

Some of us grew up in families where love was
paired with abuse and disrespect. The very people who
loved us sometimes deliberately hurt us. As adults we
may find ourselves being more decent and polite to
strangers than to our loved ones. This becomes our
adult challenge: to act respectfully to our loved ones
and protect and honor the trust they have placed in us.

*Today I will be most respectful of my intimate partner,
who is the most vulnerable to me.*

*Unknowingly we plow the dust of stars, blown about us
by the wind, and drink the universe in a glass of rain.*

—Ihab Hassan

Do we find it difficult to make conscious contact with
a Power greater than ourselves? Does the spiritual
plane seem out of reach? All we need to do is open our
consciousness to the awesome big picture. We make
contact with the ages of the universe by simply drinking a glass of water. The apple we eat is made of atoms
and molecules that have been transformed countless
times and only at this moment take the shape of an
apple. Next they will become part of our human body.

This simple mindfulness puts us in direct contact
with the vastness of space and time. Our senses taste,
smell, and feel the contact while our rational mind
simply feels awe. We were brought into being by forces
that we cannot explain, and we will be carried forward
on the wave of life. We can accept this ultimate force
and relax into it.

*Today I will be mindful of my constant contact with
powers I cannot understand.*

Two things a man should never be angry at: what he can help, and what he cannot help.

—Thomas Fuller

In the Serenity Prayer, we pray for the wisdom to know the difference between what we can change and what we cannot. That distinction can be hard for many of us to recognize. When we finally see the reality clearly— that some things we face cannot be controlled by our own will or fixed by force—new possibilities open up to us. When we stop trying to move a mountain, our relationship to the mountain changes. We start to live at peace with the mountain. At the same time we can take greater responsibility for those parts of our lives that we can change.

Peace of mind comes from accepting what we can do nothing about and taking responsibility for what we can.

Today I pray for the wisdom that helps me know the difference.

If allowed, time and nature will heal you. Remember that you do not have to heal yourself. Nature is ready to do it if you step out of her way and do not present her with those unnecessary obstacles, despair and disappointment.

—Dr. Claire Weekes

The Second Step tells us that a Power greater than ourselves can restore us to sanity. This is the hope Step. It tells us that we don't have to do it; in fact, we cannot do it ourselves. We only have to allow ourselves to receive the help that is flowing toward us right now.

Despair was a common feeling while we were caught up in our codependency and addiction. We knew no other path than to rely on ourselves, and we were defeated. The recovery path gave us a new way to go. Now we need to avoid returning to the old ways or to hopelessness. This new path calls upon us to step out of the way, welcome the healing power, and accept the hope that our recovery will proceed.

Today I will make the choice to be hopeful and accept the healing power of nature.

*The older I get, the more convinced I am that the
space between communicating human beings can
be hallowed ground.*

—Fred Rogers

When two people sit down and talk, things change.
Our true nature is basically revealed in our relationships with others. Starting from infancy, the protection
we needed to survive came through our relationships
with others. That's how we were formed into human
beings. We continue to need that connection in adult
forms for our whole lives. To be human is to be in relationship. That's where we learn to know ourselves.
That's where we grow and deepen and change. We truly
become human by the impact of our communities, our
families, our friendships, and our love relationships.

   If we carefully weigh what we let others know about
us, we remain isolated. In that state, we only recycle
our single internal conclusions over and over again.
But when we let others in and allow them to commu-
nicate with some of our best and our worst parts, we
step onto a dynamic hallowed ground with rich opportunities for growth.

*Today I will talk to someone about some of my
personal thoughts and feelings.*

*The whole life of the individual is nothing but the
process of giving birth to himself; indeed, we should be
fully born when we die.*

—Erich Fromm

We think of childhood as the period of development
and growth. For some reason we regard adulthood as
the time when we should settle down and live as fully
formed individuals. This is not true. Psychologists now
know that in a healthy person, adult development continues throughout life. When we look back five years,
we can see ways that we have changed. Life continues
to present us with new puzzles and new opportunities
to become better men.

We can also be stopped in our development if we
refuse to open up to new growth. An addiction or a
codependent way of relating to others can freeze our
growth. When we open ourselves to the truth, we can
resolve our puzzles and seize the opportunities to grow
into wiser, stronger, more generous, honest, and open-
hearted men.

*I will engage with the reality that today brings, and
I will continue to grow.*

I see God in every human being.

—Mother Teresa of Calcutta

In our spiritual development, we learn to see expressions of the creator, the ultimate good, in many places in our daily life. We may imagine that God is a distant figure that we cannot know. But many great spiritual thinkers of various religions teach us to see God within every person. That includes ourselves. We are created by God and we have a right to be here. No matter what we have done, our being is still a creation of the ultimate and we ought to hold ourselves in high esteem. When we accept this spiritual truth, what follows is that we honor ourselves and our actions express self-respect.

After we accept that God is within every fiber of our being, we can also greet all fellow human beings with honor for the God within them. This is not something that comes easily or by simple decision. It is a wisdom that grows when we come to terms with our defects and accept them as part of our whole being. We don't have to be perfect in order to honor the God within us.

Today I accept the ultimate truth of God within me and all people I see.

*Man's powers point to God, but they cannot
understand Him.*

—Reinhold Niebuhr

Our best strengths and greatest powers are signs
of God. We have been in trouble because we over-
estimated our power to control more than we could.
Now, on this spiritual path, we have turned to God,
"as we understood" God. This phrase may make us
think we have to define what this Higher Power is in
our lives. It can be helpful to think about, but we also
do well to accept the limits of our words and our
definitions.

Some guys say that they encounter God on a walk
through the forest. Some have that experience in a
church or temple. Some find God in every living crea-
ture. Most great spiritual traditions speak of God as
being present everywhere and promise that we are
never alone. The powerlessness we learn on this spiritual path includes the human impossibility to contain
God in our understanding. To encounter God, we encounter a sense of awe that God exceeds all limits.

*Today I am moved and filled with awe by the spirit
of God.*

Do, or do not. There is no "try."

—Yoda, in *The Empire Strikes Back*

Trying is what we do when we aren't willing to make a commitment. We say, "I'll try," when our heart isn't ready to give a full effort. It's what we say when we can't admit that our resolve is wimpy. And it's the lie that will defeat us.

Some challenges we face can't be conquered simply by saying, "I will do it." But we can choose to do something that will help. We can't move the mountain but we can pick up some rocks. We can engage with the problem and get to know it better. Every action we take leads somewhere and sets us up for the next action. We even learn from our mistakes and that moves us closer to achieving our goal.

Today I will not just "try"; I will do something to move toward my goal.

Everything becomes a little different as soon as it is spoken out loud.

—Hermann Hesse

Many of us find out what we really think when we start talking. Putting ideas into words is sometimes hard to do, but when we hear ourselves speak, we realize what we have had on our minds. It's an important way to go deeper into knowing ourselves. Other times we may have thoughts on our minds, but we first connect with the feelings when we say them to another person.

We are social animals and talking is a crucial part of our humanity. How often do we hear from our partners that we don't talk to them? Maybe they tell us that we "never" talk about our feelings. They love us and crave the connection that talking brings. As we become more at peace with ourselves, we can learn to express more. It takes practice, and we might need to push ourselves to put things into words, but we get even more out of it than our listeners do.

Today I will push myself to talk to my trusted friends and my partner.

All the works of God proceed slowly and in pain; but then, their roots are the sturdier and their flowering the lovelier.

—Theresa Gerhardinger

Life is difficult. No one gets through life without some struggle and pain. But we men in recovery know that our problems and struggles were the lessons that shaped us when we were willing to learn. Naturally we become impatient and want to get past the difficulties faster. We look at our neighbors who appear to have easier lives—and maybe some of them do right now. But we have our own path to walk and we must walk in our own footsteps, not someone else's.

If we had never confronted problems and pain, we would have nothing to fall back on for the next part of our life. Our transformation has already progressed. Because we keep coming back to this program and follow its guidance one day at a time, the days quickly turn into months and the months into years and our roots grow stronger.

I will live today with patience and follow the guidance that my program gives me as my transformation continues.

The greatest of all arts is the art of living together.

—William Lyon Phelps

What is this thing called intimacy? It is letting oneself be seen and known to someone who is paying attention. We all want intimacy and we often don't really know what it is. We confuse sex with intimacy. Many of us have sought the pleasure and excitement of sexual passion as the fast road to intimacy. Many of us focus on what we are looking for in a partner without looking at what we offer as a partner.

True, rewarding, and deep intimacy comes in letting ourselves be known. Sex itself is never more erotic and passionate than when we are emotionally open and honest. That doesn't mean we have license to be a jerk. We can be open and honest, and genuinely put ourselves in someone else's hands, without dumping our disrespectful or hurtful feelings on the other person. When we seek intimacy, the straight line to get there is to let ourselves be known.

Today I will let my feelings and my history be known to the one I seek intimacy with.

Approach love and cooking with reckless abandon.

—H. Jackson Brown, Jr.

Our creator made us as loving and sensuous beings. Some have said that it was our search for God, misguided though it was, that led us into addiction and codependency. Some of us have sought nirvana in a bottle, others by compulsively picking up the pieces of someone else's life, and some of us through sex, gambling, or overeating. The fact that we were misguided in our search doesn't negate the fact that we are sensuous and loving men.

We know that the very avenues to pleasure and joy can become paths to our destruction. Now we are learning to handle our emotions directly rather than by covering them with pleasure seeking. We can live a full life while guiding our search for God and for pleasure in more constructive ways. We can give free reign to our love for others without taking over their lives. We can be grown-up, sensuous, passionate lovers with our partners. We can indulge in the pleasure of great flavors without using food to cover our emotions.

Today I take great pleasure in my loves and claim my passion and sensuality.

I loved boxing. I loved every minute of it, every round in the gym, every skip of the rope, and every foot on the road. The fights were the dessert.

—Carmen Basilio, middleweight champion

Life is about the path, not just the destination. Yes, we have goals and commitments in mind; they give us direction and motivation. But getting there is our life experience. We have some big goals that guide us; they are not accomplished in a day. We live each day in the stream that carries us forward as we gradually loosen our controlling grip.

This path is about the process of moving forward as much as it is about arriving at our destination. We never use the word *cured* because we never have that much control. We only seek to be on the path and stay there, loving our experiences along the way. Once in a while we enjoy the "dessert" of an achievement, but sharing our lives with loved ones, enjoying a day of good work, taking time to go fishing or dig in the garden—these are the real stuff of a good life.

Today on my path I will take pleasure in what the day brings.

To become a father is not difficult, but to be a father is.

—Anonymous

Many of us grew up with a gap in our hearts, a longing to know our father better, to have his time, his attention, and his love. Where was he? Why did he not get more involved with us? Was his work really that important? Did he really not think about us? Did he care but just not show it?

Our father grew up with the same images of masculinity that we are dealing with: that we must keep a wall of toughness around us, that we must not show weakness or softness because someone might think less of us. Now, in our recovery and healing, we see that the unfilled yearning was part of our search that led us into problems with addiction and codependency. We were trying to satisfy our needs and soothe our pains, but without effective means. This healing journey includes making peace with our father or the memories we have of him.

Today I will accept the pain of missing my father, and I will stand on his shoulders to become a stronger, more loving man.

We didn't lose the game; we just ran out of time.

—Vince Lombardi

On a day when it seems like more things are going wrong than right, we may need to take a longer view. Today is just one day; this week is just one week on a long path. Certainly there are ups and downs on our path, and sometimes we just need more time.

We can get lost in the details of the moment, when every way we turn seems to show us more frustration. That is when we can get relief by knowing that with more time, progress will be made—and things will look different. Even when we are trying our best and we still don't see the evidence that our lives are getting better, we are actually laying the foundation of a better life.

This program of recovery holds promises for us that will be fulfilled as long as we are willing to do the work.

Today I will not be discouraged by the frustrations
I face because I believe the promise that my life will
continue to get better.

Those who are waiting are waiting very actively . . .
The secret of waiting is the faith that the seed has been
planted, that something has begun. A waiting person is
someone who is present to the moment, who believes
that this moment is the moment.

—Henri Nouwen

We know that readiness is one of the important ingredients in change. We may have heard the same thing
many times in the past, but one day, when someone
says it again, we suddenly hear it with ready ears. At
that moment, the familiar words hit their target and
we understand a deep truth for the first time.

In recovery, we don't just sit around passively waiting. We actively examine ourselves and our conscience.
We practice honesty. We make amends for our wrongs
and seek conscious contact with a Higher Power. All
these practices are ways to prepare ourselves to receive
the gifts of recovery.

Today, as I wait for the grace of God, I am actively
opening myself to receive it.

*Men can't always do what a man's gotta do to feel like
a man and still do what a man's gotta do to be a man.*

—Frank Pittman

In this program, we are living a little bit outside of the
mainstream. We are more focused on being the real
thing than on appearances. In the popular image, a
real man is self-sufficient, strong, invulnerable, able to
withstand any challenge and go it alone. Playing that
role might make us feel like a man, but we are still left
with insecurities because we know that inside we are
just putting up a front.

To be a man, we are stronger when we are big
enough to accept our weaknesses and make no excuses
for them. Of course, we don't have to bare our souls to
everyone. But we develop genuine, trusting friendships
and we are honest with ourselves and with trusted
friends. We show love to our loved ones. We may have
been taught that being vulnerable makes us not masculine. But we are amazed to find that we are more ap-
proachable and more interesting when we are genuine.

*Today I accept my vulnerabilities and my loving
feelings and allow my trusted friends to know me
as I am.*

*The tragedy of life is what dies inside a man while
he lives.*

—Albert Schweitzer

It is possible to be spiritually dead while walking
around, living and breathing. Many of us have been
there. We lost our way. Our hearts and our self-respect
were dissolved by alcohol or chemicals and we became
so involved in controlling others that we completely
lost contact with the soul at our core. But even at that
low ebb, some small glowing ember of spirit remained.

In recovery, the hot embers have been fanned back
to life. We may sense that we still have a long way to go,
but even that feeling rises from a live spirit within us.
It's never a matter of how well developed our spirituality is, but whether we are in touch with it or not. Once
we begin to have a relationship with our soul, with our
Higher Power, we are alive at our core.

Today I am grateful for the spiritual life I am leading.

Everything that irritates us about others can lead us to an understanding of ourselves.

—Carl Jung

In our worst times, we have been irritable and difficult to live with. That is common among addicts and co-dependent people. And when we feel most irritable, we are least likely to look at ourselves. It is very useful now, in recovery, when someone irritates us, to ask what inside ourselves makes us so annoyed. We often find that the very thing that irritates us about someone else is the very quality in ourselves that we don't want to face.

When another man's whining bugs us, maybe it is our own capacity for whining that we reject. When someone's self-absorption gets under our skin, maybe we are sensitive about our own self-centeredness. Sometimes we find it easier to complain about a quality in others than to admit we are like that too.

Today I will use my feelings of irritation to guide me inward and know myself better.

*I've failed over and over and over again in my life and
that is why I succeed.*

—Michael Jordan

Nobody chooses defeat. The reason we get out there
and try our best is because we want to succeed. Failure
is painful, and loss can be discouraging. To have a successful life we need to learn the techniques that successful people use to deal with failure. They know that
every attempt has its risks and that we all experience
failure. It is in our failures that we learn the most.
Everyone on the recovery path knows the pain of great
loss and the guilt of facing up to big mistakes. We also
take our failures and turn them into net gain by learning the lessons they contain.

Our strength for the future of our lives comes, in
part, from mining the resources to be found in the
rubble of failure. We refine those resources by our honesty about them. Our experience with what worked
and what didn't work points the way to a stronger,
wiser life. When we demand resilience from ourselves,
we rebound from failure to step forward toward success with our next venture.

*Today I accept that every failure contains the seeds for
success in the future.*

November

□ □ □ □ □ □ □

There's a lot of credit that can be given to youth and enthusiasm, but with them comes foolishness. Age and craftsmanship is not to be played down. I have got more tricks up my sleeves than an alligator has teeth.

—George Foreman

As men in the early stages of recovery, we often have felt that we were walking on rubber legs. We felt very shaky. We were ready to admit that our lives had become unmanageable, but to establish a more stable life seemed like an overwhelming challenge. We needed the support of others in the program who were ahead of us on this path. So we turned to our sponsors and to other people in our meetings who had walked these Steps before us.

As men who have longer sobriety, we know that we need to share our stories and help others to maintain our own lifesaving recovery. So we continue to attend our meetings as one part of our maintenance program. We become sponsors and share our tricks of recovery because it benefits us as much as the other guy.

Today, as a newcomer to recovery, or as one with more time in, I know that we all have a lot to give.

It is not the employer who pays—he only handles the
money. It is the product that pays wages.

—Henry Ford

Our work gives us meaning and can be the source of
many good feelings. Even when we wish we had a better job, we feel good when we do the job we have well.
Sometimes at work we get caught up in resentments or
personal feelings that tear down our self-esteem. The
best tonic for negative feelings at work is to focus on
doing a good job, regardless of all the other issues we
have to deal with.

Whether we are building complex technical equip-
ment, cutting meat, or managing a team, the product
we turn out is the bottom line. It expresses our character. In the long run, an excellent performance will
come back to reward us. Knowing that we gave it our
best is a source of inner pride.

Today I know that self-respect comes from doing my
job well.

Change and growth take place when a person has
risked himself and dares to become involved with
experimenting with his life.

—Herbert Otto

On our path, we take the unique circumstances that
life presents and seek ways to use them in positive
ways. Our path is long, with many turns and bends
that lead beyond what we can see in advance. The most
cautious person might hold back from the unknown
and try desperately to control the future. Risk-taking is
an important ingredient in good mental health because it opens possibilities to us that the safest choices
will never give us.

We have taken unwise risks in the past and now we
are tempted, in recovery, to hold tightly to safety. But a
balanced life calls us to take constructive risks. We
might risk asking someone to be our sponsor, even
when we don't know how he will respond. We might
risk letting ourselves fall more deeply in love than we
have ever been before. We might risk telling a friend
about a long-held secret, simply to let him know us
better. We might risk applying for a job that will challenge us. There is room for us to try something, miss
our mark, and still learn from the experience.

Today I will feel the thrill and excitement of taking
a constructive risk.

*Darkness cannot drive out darkness; only light can do
that. Hate cannot drive out hate; only love can do that.*

—Dr. Martin Luther King, Jr.

What darkness do we feel in our lives today? Are we
troubled by a relationship? Is guilt about past mistakes
clouding our peace of mind? Do we feel threatened by
a challenge that looms before us? Perhaps we live with
an illness or we feel trapped by our life's circumstances.
Darkness is universal. It is one side of the coin of life.

We cannot not respond to this darkness. The question always is, how will we respond? Many times our
established ways of responding to our situation only
perpetuate the problem. So we must now seek a way to
respond differently. We can do the counterintuitive
thing. If we can forgive ourselves, it is easier to forgive
others. If we first calm ourselves in the face of challenge instead of letting ourselves panic, we will bring
our better self to cope with it. If we respond to anger
and hate with genuine loving honesty, we may change
the nature of a relationship. Light and love are also
universal, and we can choose to walk in the light.

*Today I will respond with calmness and a loving frame
of mind.*

The will to win means nothing without the will to prepare.

—Juma Ikangaa, Tanzanian runner

Recovery and healing are not a matter of triumphantly grasping victory in our hands, no matter how much we might want to do that. Rather, our part is the hard work of getting ourselves ready to receive the healing that comes to us. The Twelve Steps are the work of preparing ourselves. We can work at learning what it means to surrender; we can work at taking personal inventory—and these things help prepare us.

The healing comes when we are ready, not as something we bought and paid for, but as a gift in response to being ready.

Today I will continue to work to ready myself to receive the gifts of recovery.

*That is the thankless position of the father in the
family—the provider for all, and the enemy of all.*

—August Strindberg

Many of us feel like outsiders in our families. We sometimes feel like a paycheck and not much more to our
loved ones. We grew up with absent fathers and we
never learned how to live as fathers in the close circle of
love at home.

How can we move from an outsider position—or
even an enemy position—into a full partnership with
our mates and families? We can begin by showing our
real selves. We take the risk of telling them what we
care about, what we love, and how we feel. We say what
scares us, what breaks our hearts, and what our past
was like. The greatest gift we can give is to open our
feelings and let our loved ones know us.

These changes do not happen in a day or even a
month. But gradually, with repeated expressions of
ourselves, in the process of letting ourselves be known,
we become loved for who we are, not only for what we
can do.

Today I will tell someone in my family how I feel.

Truly, when the need is greatest, then God's help is always nearest. Should we not willingly offer our hands and heart where help is still possible?

—Theresa Gerhardinger

In the Twelfth Step of our recovery program, we tell our stories to others who need to hear that there is hope. As we live in our circle of recovering people, we can lose sight of the fact that more people still die of their addictions than recover. We never forget how dismal and futile life becomes in the grip of addiction and codependency, and how desperately we needed a way out. By the grace of God, help was there for us. Now we find meaning and spiritual growth by telling our stories of hope to others.

We still can slip into dark moods and self-pity. That is when we benefit most from reaching out, not so much to get help as to pass it on to those who need help. Sometimes the help we give is by inviting someone to come with us to a meeting. Other times we can give help by mentoring a young child, donating food to hungry people, visiting old people who are lonely, or volunteering at our community celebration.

Today I will look for ways to reach out to others in need.

*Remember that great love and great achievements
involve great risk.*

—H. Jackson Brown, Jr.

We are not strangers to risk. Many of us have taken
huge risks in our addictions and codependency. Looking back at what we put at risk sometimes makes us
cringe. Now, in recovery, we may instinctively pull back
from any risk. But any good thing can be taken too far.
If we refused to take any risk, we'd never fall in love,
we'd never reach out a helping hand to someone in
need, we'd never take on a project that might yield big
rewards.

Our recovery and our willingness to turn our lives
over to the care of our Higher Power is an adventure
that leads us in unknown directions. The spiritual
path is one with interesting and surprising turns. The
decision part of turning it over is only the beginning.
The next thing we need to learn is to relax and feel
comfortable when we are not grabbing control. It takes
time and repeated lapses; but each time we return to
our trust in God.

*Today I will move forward, not knowing where this
path leads, trusting that things will turn out okay.*

Other things may change us, but we start and end with family.

—Anthony Brandt

In our childhoods, our families formed our self-image and our understanding of what relationships are. We learned to either have trust in the system of intimacy that nurtured us, or to distrust the fibers of those close bonds. For some of us it is easier to trust relationships that aren't close than to feel trust after they become close. Many of us become more fearful and anxious with someone after we are deeply involved with them because we were formed in childhood to feel wary.

As adults, we are still developing and changing. No one reaches adulthood fully formed. Some of us have been stuck in our childhood state. But we are not limited to what we learned as children if we are willing to be challenged to grow in adult love. We have to give ourselves some slack when we make mistakes; there is always room for repair. And we have to grant the same to our loved ones. When we are willing to be honest about our feelings and willing to hear what our loved ones are telling us, we will continue to become better men.

Today I continue my adult development to become a better man.

Patience and passage of time do more than strength and fury.

—Jean de la Fontaine

It's part of our masculine style: when we see a problem, we want to get out our tool kit and fix it. We admire strength and the ability to remedy any problem. That's not always bad, but as we get older and wiser we learn that not everything can be fixed with a hammer.

Masculine strength and aggressiveness don't solve all problems. A savvy man who has been around the block a few times learns other approaches to problems. We learn that patience and timing are incredible forces for accomplishing great things. As we continue to focus on our own recovery and transformation, sometimes we feel impatient for the rewards and the peace of mind that are promised in this program. The best remedy for impatience is to turn our attention back to the challenges and the rewards that this particular day brings. They are sufficient for us to deal with.

Today I will remember that time is my friend and is working on my side.

A truth that's told with bad intent
Beats all the lies you can invent.

—William Blake

Sometimes the truth is the most brutal thing we can deliver. In our recovery we work very hard to become honest with ourselves, but we must also learn how to handle the truth with others. We are guided to make amends to all those we have harmed, "except when to do so would injure them or others." We must consider our motivations for expressing the truth and see that sometimes privacy and silence isn't dishonest; it's respectful.

The man who apologized to a married couple for his affair with the wife did no one any good by his apology. The man who freely gossips about others may speak the truth, but he only gratifies his selfish urges. We are learning to be clear and unflinching in our honesty with ourselves, and gentle and constructive in our honesty with others.

Today I will tell the truth in caring and respectful ways.

All self-knowledge is purchased at the cost of guilt.

—Paul Tillich

When we take our searching and fearless moral inventory, we walk directly into our feelings of guilt. We have done wrong and hurt people and there is no longer any hiding from it. That is why we are called to be fearless in our search. A great reward follows our admission, and that reward is the chance to know ourselves and make peace with ourselves.

When we get honest with ourselves about the effects of our actions, we feel the pain that we avoided by denial. It was somehow easier to hide and escape than to stand up to the truth. When we stand up to the responsibility for our actions and their effects on others and ourselves, we actually stand taller and feel more self-respect. Guilt itself is not a bad thing, but holding on to it and leaving it unrepaired is. We may not have known that we were buying something very precious by facing our guilt.

Today I will face my responsibilities for my actions and receive the benefits of knowing myself better.

Oh God, help me to believe the truth about myself—no matter how beautiful it is.

—Macrina Wiederkehr

We struggle with low confidence and poor self-images. When we try to get honest with ourselves, we often find it easier to see the negative things about ourselves than the positive. A searching and fearless inventory often means admitting the bad stuff. But an equal or greater challenge is to admit the good stuff. If we are to be truly honest, if we are to know ourselves well, we must admit our strengths and our highest qualities. We must not be blind to the best aspects of ourselves.

When we look deep inside, perhaps we find a kind heart toward children. Maybe we have reached out to friends when they needed someone. Some of us have been reliable as good providers, even through our worst trouble. All of us have our own unique good qualities to claim, and our journey calls us to be honest about them.

Today I can name and accept some good qualities in myself.

We know what a person thinks, not when he tells us what he thinks, but by his actions.

—Isaac Bashevis Singer

Until we gain enough self-awareness, we may mistake our words for the truth. Many of us have developed patterns of self-deception to serve our addictions and codependency. It's as if we believe that if we can make it sound good, it must be true. And if we are good with words, we can make almost any choice or any action sound good, especially to ourselves. We also value the approval of others so we are tempted to say the "right" thing even if it doesn't match what is in our hearts.

As we grow stronger, we value honesty with ourselves more deeply. We have greater self-esteem and we no longer betray or deceive ourselves. We learn to discern the difference between "just words" and the truth spoken from our hearts. Our words no longer cover our actions or substitute for them; our words help us better understand our actions. Words can now be used to express and clarify what we do.

Today my words will express and clarify my actions, not obscure them.

Hope begins in the dark, the stubborn hope that if you just show up and try to do the right thing, the dawn will come.

—Anne Lamott

Darkness is no stranger to any adult. Some of us know all too well how dark some nights can seem. Many of us in our darkest hours have even considered ending our lives. At those times we feel totally alone and don't see any hope remaining. And yet we keep putting one foot in front of the other, feeling no hope except the hope that we will find hope. The small flickering light of stubborn hope continues to burn.

Even when we cannot see the light, dawn always comes. It doesn't come when we want it to. It doesn't arrive when we feel we deserve it. Dawn comes on its own time. What we are required to do is to keep showing up.

Today I will keep putting one foot in front of the other, knowing that darkness and light are part of the rhythm of life.

Slump? I ain't in no slump . . . I just ain't hitting.

—Yogi Berra

Flat times in our lives require a bigger perspective. Sometimes we can't pinpoint what is wrong, except that we don't have our usual spirit. We get up in the morning and life seems drab even while the sun smiles through the window. Other times we know that we have good reason to not be "hitting." Ups and downs are natural parts of life.

In the past, we used alcohol, drugs, and other addictive behaviors to escape the feelings of a slump. We never allowed ourselves to feel sad, lonely, or empty, or to even get acquainted with what our feelings were all about. But in a healthy, more grown-up life we make room for slumps. We know they aren't permanent, we can tolerate them, and we will feel better later.

We gain perspective by living through it. While walking along a rough path, keeping one eye on the middle distance helps to steady our balance. We know that we have felt better in the past, and we will feel better again.

Today I will stay on the path.

Any soldier who has been in combat knows that there comes a time after battle, when the smoke has blown away and the dust has settled, when you must lean over and give your foe a hand. For in that moment of generosity, the war is truly over.

—Frederick Downs, Jr.

Forgiveness is a healing act for both the giver and receiver. It transforms us from unhappy, angry men holding on to old resentments into men who are freed of the past and ready to live at peace in the present.

Forgiveness doesn't mean forgetting. It means that we simply let go of feeling that someone owes us something for past wrongs. It means we write off the bad debts of previous events. Old foes can sometimes even become friends. The foe may have inspired a secret sense of respect in us: how well he fought! We could even say he was a worthy foe and now he can become our respected friend.

What we couldn't see well at close range may become clearer with the distance of time. Personal growth in recovery calls us to name our old enemies and work toward the forgiveness that rewards us with peace of mind.

Today I will live in the spirit of forgiveness.

Willingness to accept responsibility for one's life is the source from which self-respect springs.

—Joan Didion

We all know the struggle with shame and self-blame. It is a painful issue and has often been the source of many other bad choices. When we don't think we are very important, we may dismiss relationships with others as meaningless; we disappear from them and cause great harm in the process. We make self-defeating choices because we feel that we don't really matter anyway. It's possible to remain in this state of low self-esteem for years, feeling mystified about how to gain a better self-image.

The truth is both quite simple and challenging. When we hold values and live by them, we respect ourselves. This doesn't require perfection. It requires that when we make mistakes or fall short of our values, we admit it. By so doing we reaffirm our respect for our values even though, this time, our actions didn't match them. In this way we remember that who we are is not the same as what we do.

Today I will take responsibility for my actions.

Nothing is more desirable than to be released from an affliction, but nothing is more frightening than to be divested of a crutch.

—James Baldwin

We don't realize how attached we are to something until we lose it. Even our burdens can be the focus of our lives. When we have the affliction of addiction, we don't want all the problems it creates: the financial woes, the disrupted relationships, or the sick and tired feelings. In our codependency we have relied on our ability to control situations and pick up the pieces after others messed up. But it's very frightening to give up what was our escape. We wonder what we will do with our time and where we will turn for comfort.

Everything changes when we see this fear as a spiritual problem. In our addiction mode we responded from the impulsive part of our brain. Without rationality, we impulsively reached for comfort and pleasure. Now the spiritual path shows us a new alternative. Our fears about giving up our crutch are fears that we will not be safe and comfortable. With a relationship to the God of our understanding, we can rely on a Higher Power to care for anything we fear.

Today I will not impulsively react to my anxiety. Instead I will turn it over to my Higher Power and walk confidently forward.

A life lived in fear is a life half lived.

—Roma proverb

Facing our fears is part of our spiritual development. First we must admit them. We were raised to be dishonest about our fear, to betray our own consciousness by saying we were not afraid. When we get honest, we see how many things we have avoided, how often we felt tense and uneasy, all because we were afraid. We worry that there won't be enough to fill our needs, that we will be alone, that we won't survive a difficult time. But something mystical happens when we learn at a deep level to turn what we cannot control over to the care of God.

For most of us, we don't absorb this mystery all at once, then live without fear. It is something we keep returning to. We worry about a speech we have to make . . . and then we remember to turn it over to God and feel peaceful again. We worry about a trip we will be taking . . . and then come back to our spiritual peace. We worry about the health of a loved one . . . and then turn it over. This spiritual practice is a centerpiece of our healing journey.

Today I will keep returning to the peace that comes when I turn the future over to the care of God.

The breeze at dawn has secrets to tell you. You must ask for what you want. Don't go back to sleep.

—Rumi

We were asleep and now we are awake. The breeze that woke us may have been sharp and biting, but it was a gift that brought us back to consciousness. We carry many wants in our hearts. We needed to wake up to remember them.

On this particular day, we can remind ourselves of the things we want most and ask our Higher Power to keep us on our path to find them. It is good to take an inventory of our deepest desires. Most of all we want the healing and recovery that makes all other things possible. Many of us want to be good fathers to our children. We want to feel love and be good partners to our intimate mate. We want to be productive and fulfill our abilities and talents. We want to be good and strong and generous men.

Today I am grateful for my awakening to this renewed life.

It is our choices . . . that show what we truly are, far more than our abilities.

—J. K. Rowling

Intelligence, talent, skill, achievement, and wealth are wonderful assets. But we all know people with these assets whom we don't admire. The man we most admire is the one who plays a bad hand well. No matter how smart or limited a guy may be, how physically strong or weak, or how high or low his job is, what we admire most in a guy is how he deals with his circumstances.

Our task today is to make the choices that we respect most, rather than the choices that only serve our hungry egos. We can cultivate a generous, tolerant, self-respecting character by choosing attitudes and actions to express these traits. We can welcome newcomers, forgive those who have hurt us, include those who are different from us, and be generous to everyone. When we follow that path, we will have the pleasure of friendship and the rewards of self-fulfillment.

Today I will choose actions that express my best self.

*The self is not something ready-made, but something
in continuous formation through choice of action.*

—John Dewey

We're not the men we used to be. The little boy who
went off to his first day of school so many years ago exists only as a memory. The guy who pursued his controlling behaviors and sought his pleasures and escapes
is not the guy who now follows a path of healing and
recovery. We build upon who we were and the experiences we had, and we continue our formation into a
whole self as long as we live. That is why we continue
through daily prayer and meditation to look at ourselves and make the choices that will take us further in
the direction of a stronger, more self-respecting man.

Some of us were frozen in our development and
didn't continue to grow in our wisdom and emotional
strength. We were seduced by the allure of childish answers and easy escapes from the challenges in our lives.
Our formation as adult men was sidetracked and
bogged down, going nowhere. Now we have made new
choices that put us back on the track that continues
our growth.

*Today I choose to stay on course to live the life that
restores me.*

What is to give light must endure burning.

—Viktor Frankl

We all are born into a life that inevitably includes some amount of challenge, pain, and distress mixed with the joy and learning. Our strength and our wisdom grow by dealing with trouble. The wisest people we know—the ones we admire most—have life stories that brought them through dark days of despair and striking difficulties. Their trial by fire sharpened their clarity about what really counts in life and raised their motivation to live by their values.

Life has become better for us in recovery. But no one ever becomes immune to life's problems. We get stronger and wiser in dealing with them. We get better at maintaining our balance when everything seems to push us off balance. As we grow more skilled in dealing with life, our light shines on the path for others seeking their way.

Today I accept that difficulty is part of life, and I will learn what it has to teach me.

Gratitude is heaven itself.

—William Blake

The feeling of gratefulness sometimes sweeps over us and fills us with a warm glow. We know what it feels like to be lost and frightened, with no compass to point our way out. The great contrast between where we once were and where we are today inspires us to feel thankful. Now we have our lives back. We feel like real men again. We have the companionship of fine people. We have hope for the future.

This feeling of gratitude is an antidote to our struggles with desire. Our desires have taken us places that harmed us. We wanted more control, we wanted more pleasure, we wanted our feelings to stop, and we wanted more than was good for us. We have enough right now. This fullness of gratitude is a wonderful relief from our driving desires.

Today my desires are set aside by my gratitude and the knowledge that I have enough.

Experience is what you get when you don't get what you want.

—Dan Stanford

We want what we want and we often feel entitled to it, but it's only when reality gives us something else that we get pushed into further growth. We may have a road map to our destination, but if we have car trouble on the way, we will have some unexpected experiences. Our first response to a change in plans is usually frustration or disappointment. We never would have chosen to face the situation. But facing it changes us and we become a different person. Often the change is small, but some events change us in big ways forever.

That is why we are only partly in control of the course our life will take. After we have changed, we become loyal to the new person we are becoming. We appreciate what we learned. When we choose responses that match our integrity, we come out stronger, wiser, and more experienced.

Today I will be open to the experiences that I didn't plan.

If called by a panther
Don't anther.

—Ogden Nash

We were brought to this program after following our desires and our passions to self-destructive extremes. Sometimes we still hear the call from that dark side, seducing us back to the ecstatic highs. Relapse is always a danger. We never get over being addicts and codependents. No man eradicates his dark side. It's not a bridge we can burn behind us.

How do we prevent the ever-possible relapse? First, we accept that we cannot fight tomorrow's battles today, so we don't worry about how we will stay clean and sober in the future. That eliminates our worry about tomorrow's sobriety. Second, we keep our connection open with other people. We stay in touch with them. We keep talking and don't allow ourselves to fall back into old patterns of isolation. When we hear that seductive call, we talk to others about it. And third, we take our mistakes and turn them into something productive by learning from them.

Today, once again, I admit that I am a codependent and/or an addict and that my recovery is a daily process of healing.

Like all young men, I set out to be a genius, but mercifully laughter intervened.

—Laurence Durrell

Self-centeredness is a remnant from our immature past. In that remnant is our inclination to take ourselves too seriously. When we can laugh at our mistakes rather than be ashamed of them, we have come a long way. When we can shed the burden of "specialness," our load is remarkably lighter. When we can let another person's sarcasm reflect back on him rather than allow it into our core, our relationships are simpler and easier. When we can simply participate rather than needing to be the top dog, we have a lot more fun. When we can accept compliments with gratitude and be a humble winner, we like ourselves better.

In our manhood we strive to achieve, not so that we are better than everyone else, but so that we can fulfill our potential. We want to be the best person we can be, not the best person in our group. We aren't driven to overcome our shame by being perfect. We accept our imperfection as part of universal human nature and accept that we are all more alike than we are different. Competition can be fun; it doesn't have to put our self-esteem on the line.

Today I will laugh at myself and take joy in being human.

Too many people are thinking of security instead of opportunity. They seem more afraid of life than death.

—James F. Byrnes

Life is never fully secure, and those of us who grew up in stressful households learned early that security was a precious thing. What we didn't learn was how to reach out from our security to seek and grasp opportunity. One problem we may develop in our recovery is overcautiousness, which comes out of our frightening memories of being out of control in our addiction and codependency.

Life is always a risk. Walking up to the plate to take a swing at the next pitch is a risk, but life is so much richer for doing so. Part of our recovery is learning to accept opportunity when it appears and allow for the possibility of mistake. We don't need to condemn ourselves for having tried; we can learn from every attempt. We are much more alive for the risks we take and the opportunities we accept.

Today my life is richer for the possibilities that I am moving toward.

I don't know the key to success but the key to failure is trying to please everyone.

—Bill Cosby

In our codependency we often think first about what others want. We try to make everyone happy and smooth the edges of conflict for everyone else. It seems like such a caring and loving way to live. We may even be so grandiose as to think we can handle frustrations and swallow disappointments better than others can. Whatever created this urge within us, when we take it to extremes, we are so focused on others that we don't even know our own feelings. Sometimes we act in dishonest ways to protect others and we get blamed for the failures that inevitably result.

In recovery we develop the humility to understand that we are members of the human race, no stronger than others, no better able to care for others than they can for themselves. Happiness comes from within each person; we cannot create it in them. Our own peace of mind comes from within us, not from pleasing others. If someone is disappointed in us, we are big enough to accept that. Our first obligation is to take responsibility for ourselves, then we can begin to be generous toward others.

Today I will know myself first and accept that I don't have to please everyone.

December

Even if you are on the right track, you'll get run over if you just sit there.

—Will Rogers

No matter when we started walking this recovery path, we always need to return to the questions: What Step am I focusing on today? What lessons do I need to learn from these events in my life? There is a natural ebb and flow in the focus of our spiritual lives. Sometimes we awaken and become highly alert to our life development; other times we are sleepier about it. We cannot afford to go to sleep in our spiritual and character development.

It has been asked of people after they relapsed, what Step were you working just before you relapsed? Usually the true answer is no Step at all. They have fallen asleep on the path. There is no cure for addiction or codependency. It is a permanent condition. So we need to keep walking the Steps.

Today I will stay on track by renewing my focus on my growth.

I can accept failure, but I can't accept not trying.

—Michael Jordan

Sometimes failure can be a trap that, if we let it, stops us in our development. We get discouraged and absorb failure as if it defined us. We may indulge in self-pity and wrap ourselves in the "loser" label. It's a painful identity, but there's a payoff: we rationalize that there's no point in risking again, so we won't need to put forth any more effort. That kind of choice is like a hiding place for our true self. We cannot afford to indulge in such hiding places.

On this path, hiding and self-pity only freeze our growth. We must learn to deal with failure as a part of life. We are human and that means we are incomplete as long as we live. We must accept that we will fail at many things on the way to finding achievement. If we block failure, we block success. So our true identity is that of learner, seeker, and adventurer—a man who rebounds from failure and comes back with his best shot.

Today I will fulfill my true self and learn from whatever happens.

Sometimes it is more important to discover what one cannot do than what one can do.

—Lin Yutang

There was a time for each of us when we had not yet discovered important truths about what we could not do. Until we had uncovered this knowledge, we could not take the first Step. We were doomed to stay locked in a cycle that led nowhere but down. No matter how much we tried to improve our self-esteem, no matter how many awards or salary raises we got, we were going nowhere with our personal life. We first needed to learn that we could not control some things.

Once we read the unhappy news that we could not control our addictive behaviors, and we could not control others, we were ready to take the first Step. Then a whole world opened up to us. Only then were we ready to learn what we could do. Even now we use that experience as a model for our lives. When we accept what we cannot control, our understanding of the problem changes, we become calmer, and new possibilities come into view.

Today I am prepared to learn from discovering what I cannot control.

No one can make you feel inferior without your consent.

—Eleanor Roosevelt

When we are oversensitive, when we take offense at a negative comment someone makes to us, we put our self-esteem under that person's control. Whatever a person says is, first of all, a reflection on him. If someone says you look like a pig, that doesn't make it so. Children don't have the inner resources or the emotional independence to hold a separate identity apart from what others say, and they can be crushed by it. Adolescents take great personal offense if someone looks at them wrong. As adults, we have the ability to control our sense of self, even if we haven't yet learned how to use it.

If our partner speaks in a tone that sounds judgmental, our knee-jerk response is to take it into our core. If a co-worker hurls an insult, we might feel injured. If a friend is thoughtless about our feelings, we might take offense. But we can remember that these actions are first of all a reflection on the speaker. We can adopt a detached attitude about others' comments and give them the freedom to say what they like. We are in charge of our self-esteem.

My honesty about my own self-worth stands on its own. No one else controls that.

Our minds go racing about like horses running wild in the fields, while our emotions remain unmanageable, like monkeys swinging in the trees.

—Dogen Zenji

When we follow the guidance to pray and meditate every day, we see how busy our minds and emotions are. Often we react out of our emotions, not even knowing we are doing so and believing we are totally rational. The wildness of our inner world is universal and human. Our development as men means taming those horses and monkeys, making friends with them, and training them to work for us rather than running off in all directions.

We grow by getting to know our feelings and thoughts. Emotions are no longer a mystery to us. We can talk about them and express them to trusted friends. After we have come to know what we feel and think, we are less at their mercy and less likely to react on impulse. We know what we are dealing with and we can choose how we will respond.

Today I am getting to know those wild horses and monkeys in my mind.

Character is what you know you are, not what others think you are.

—Marva Collins and Civia Tamarkin

True self-esteem is built by having values and living by them. Many men seek to repair their self-esteem by going after the praise of others. Praise is nice to get, but the most highly successful men can still live with an insatiable hunger, an empty hole in their own self-regard.

Our self-esteem is built by first asking ourselves what our values are. What do we admire most in a man? What do we believe is most important in the character of a good person? What is our highest calling as we live our lives? When we have the answers to these kinds of questions, we have a road map to achieving an inner feeling that we are worthwhile. We don't have to be perfect in fulfilling those values, but if we use them as our guides, we will have self-esteem, regardless of whether others praise us.

Today I will choose my actions in accord with my highest values.

All action ends in passion because the response to our
action is out of our hands. That is the mystery of work,
the mystery of love, the mystery of friendship, the
mystery of community—they always involve waiting.

—Henri Nouwen

In our desire for control, we want to not only say the
right thing but control how it is heard. We want to
take an action and have others respond just as we
planned. But the spiritual path takes us into the mystery where we accept the truth of what we do not control. We would do well to think of ourselves as an
archer. To shoot an arrow, we have to let it go.

We can do our best to say what we sincerely believe
and then let others listen and respond. We can do what
we believe is the right action and then wait for others
to take it where they choose. That is the only authentic
dialogue. Our faith comes into play when we engage in
the dialogue, knowing that we can only say and do our
half of the exchange. Out of the process something
real will emerge.

Today I will live in the mystery of my life, let go of the
responses to my actions, and simply wait.

The day you were born a ladder was set up to help you escape this world.

—Rumi

In a spiritual life, as our soul develops, our consciousness reaches beyond the mundane world of things, events, and facts. We find meaning in the happenings of our lives: a chance meeting with a friend, a rainstorm that changes our plans, or even our simple daily chores. And we find our connection to the larger whole through friendships and community. We care, we love, and our actions fulfill our sense of who we want to be as men.

Many of us have outgrown or turned away from the religious training we received as boys. Others of us grew within the religions of our childhoods, developing adult spiritual lives. In either case, spiritual development is the process of discovering or uncovering what was there for us, perhaps what was meant for us, from the day we were born.

Today I am in touch with my soul.

It has been my philosophy of life that difficulties vanish when faced boldly.

—Isaac Asimov

When a serious problem comes into our life, the first question most of us ask is, why me?

It's a question with no answer. But we know that being born means we will face problems and challenges. No life is free of them. Our development is as much about learning to deal with problems as it is about learning to avoid them. Most of us have tried mightily to *not* deal with our problems by hiding from them or denying them. We have also tried bulldozing our way over problems with the force of our will.

Now we have a new tool for facing problems; it's the paradox of powerlessness. Now we understand that we cannot control many of life's challenges. When we boldy face difficulties that we cannot control, we accept the facts. Accepting our powerlessness over a problem surprisingly makes us stronger. It changes everything. It even transforms our life.

Today I will face difficulty head on and admit the situation as I see it.

What comes from the heart goes to the heart.

—Samuel Taylor Coleridge

Most of what we say and do is laden with implication and feeling. We can say the same words with many different inflections and convey very different meanings. When we have something very important to say, we may worry whether we will be understood. We can rely on the truth that when we speak from our heart to a trusted friend, and when we have his attention, our message will strike a chord.

A man was worried about speaking at a meeting. His friend told him, "Say it from the heart, man! Say it from the heart!" Communication at that level is instantly clear. We all have things in our hearts that we may be afraid to say. We can say them if we remind ourselves that a message from the heart will be heard by the heart. As we grow in our strength and recovery, we become more comfortable and we speak more and more from that level.

Today I will keep my heart open and speak to others from that level.

The Eskimo term for sexual intercourse is "laughing together."

—Anonymous

This Eskimo term teaches us that sexuality is a God-given gift intended to bring pleasure and create bonds between two people. Problems surrounding sexuality are common among recovering men, and it is another area where we can grow. Some of us attached great anxiety to sex and used chemicals to handle our anxiety. In sobriety we become faced with the anxiety again. Some of us used sex as our drug, an addiction that served more to escape our feelings than to enrich them.

Our sexual desires and feelings provide energy for our intimate partnership. There is no more shame in having a sexual problem than there is in having a communication problem with someone. We can learn that taking sexual pleasure within a loving relationship is hardly separate from giving it. Talking to our intimate partner and a trusted friend can relieve many problems. Just as we can lighten the burden of any other problem, sexual matters are solvable too.

Today I am grateful for the pleasure and the gift of sexuality.

There are some defeats more triumphant than victories.

—Michel de Montaigne

The spiritual path is filled with paradox. One example is the word *defeat*, which has a bad reputation. In recovery we learn that brokenness can be the beginning of changes for the better. Sometimes the drive of our ego takes us on a very exciting but destructive ride. Only in defeat do we open our eyes and begin to understand the deeper truth and go in a direction that fits our better self. That is every man's story in recovery. Out of defeat we find a new form of triumph.

This may be a day in which we face particular worries or losses. Our first thoughts are about the pain and difficulty—we don't yet know what we need to learn from them. We only need to stay focused on the kind of man we choose to be. From that will come the wisdom and the wherewithal to create the kind of life we will feel good about.

Today I am grateful for the sustaining power of this spiritual life and will stay focused on the kind of man I choose to be.

The real voyage of discovery consists not in seeking new landscapes but in having new eyes.

—Marcel Proust

We have awakened with new eyes as men with new lives. We are walking in the same world but seeing it with new clarity. We were asleep in the darkness, pursuing pleasures that ultimately brought only pain and pursuing control over that which could not be controlled. What once was confusing and beyond the grasp of our understanding we now find simple and interesting in the bright sunlight of our new lives. This path of healing is based on honesty with ourselves and acceptance of our powerlessness.

On this path we feel like real human beings. We may see that we have much work to do, but we have hope for our lives. Healing has become an exciting adventure. We are gaining a sense of self-esteem, our friendships are deeper, and we are more productive at work. When we feel discouraged, we have new choices for handling our feelings.

Today I am grateful to be awake and to see the world with new eyes.

*Man is the only kind of varmint who sets his own trap,
baits it, and then steps in it.*

—John Steinbeck

It's a universal truth that we often reap the results of
our own bad choices. We are drawn to substances and
behaviors that seem so pleasurable at first, but lead us
far astray from the kind of man we want to be. Our bad
choices may be self-indulgent escapes from the challenges of life. Ultimately the escape becomes the trap.
We are in the company of millions of would-be escap-
ers, but some of us did a bigger job of it than others.

Life as a spiritual path means that we learn from
our mistakes and we get better at facing our challenges
head-on. There is no need to berate ourselves for being
human. When we learn from our experience, it isn't a
total loss, and we grow deeper.

*Today I am grateful for what I have already learned,
and I will keep an open mind to continue to learn
from my mistakes.*

A problem is a chance for you to do your best.

—Duke Ellington

The nature of life is that we are consistently faced with problems. We don't directly choose the puzzle that presents itself to us, but we choose how we will respond to it. The puzzles we get and the responses we choose shape the kind of man we become. Some of us are tempted to balk at our circumstances and refuse to deal with them. We get stuck on the idea that it isn't fair for us to have our particular problem, and we want to quit trying.

Sometimes, facing the fact that we cannot change a problem and accepting it is the highest form of character. Other times, digging deep within ourselves to pull up the best we can muster and facing a difficult challenge turns us into a better man than we knew we could be. The challenge itself is the inspiration that brings out our best.

Today I will accept the problems I face and give them the best I can muster.

You must do the thing you cannot do.

—Eleanor Roosevelt

We are faced with what we cannot do. We are up against a stone wall. A fundamental wisdom about adulthood is that we have not grown up until we grasp our powerlessness and accept its lessons. Easy answers from the immature and inexperienced tell us to buck up, never give in, and do it alone. Every adult faces this wall in his life, whether he is an addict or codependent or not. If he hasn't faced it or doesn't accept it, he has not yet truly grown into manhood.

When we have tried every tactic and every control maneuver to manage what we cannot change, there is another option. We can accept that we are powerless to change the stone wall. This acceptance feels like defeat at first. But it also makes us wiser and leads to deeper insight about life. In the Twelve Step program, surrender is only the first Step to a new beginning. We are next led to a spiritual connection that makes the impossible possible. Out of the collapse of our old ways can rise a new way of life—and a new man.

Today I am grateful that I was guided out of despair into new possibilities.

Until you are willing to let go of your parents, you continue to conceive of yourself as a child.

—Frederick Perls

Emancipation is a lot more than living away from our parents and supporting ourselves. Many things can still hold us within the limitations of childhood. Some of us haven't shaken the criticisms we heard as children. Some of still turn to indulgent parents who pick up the pieces and don't expect us to stand on our own two feet. Some of us hold onto resentments about our parents. These things imprison us within our expired childhood.

By its nature, emancipation cannot be handed to us. It is only won by taking it—by our own maturity. Letting go of our parents means we choose to be grown up and independent. We tear up the I.O.U. and go forward into manhood. After letting our parents go, we can have adult relationships with them and enjoy them for who they are.

Today I am letting go of my parents so that I can live in the present as an adult man.

*If you are patient in one moment of anger, you will
escape a hundred days of sorrow.*

—Chinese proverb

Anger is a life force. It gives us energy and motivation.
Like so many other things, it is not inherently good or
evil. The key for us, as developing men, is how we use
our anger.

We can all recall times when we felt the power of
anger but handled our feelings badly. We popped off
impulsively and were filled with regret. Or maybe we
couldn't admit our mistake and went to extremes to
justify our bad behavior. Some of us have been so
frightened by our own anger or someone else's that
now we avoid it at all costs.

As adult men we develop good ways to manage this
power. We start by getting acquainted with anger so
that we know it when it shows up. We aren't ruled by it
and we aren't afraid to feel anger. This Chinese proverb
doesn't say to hide from anger. It says to begin with patience. Then we can form an effective way to handle
anger so that we won't have regrets.

*Today I will accept my feelings of anger when they
arise, and I will express them in constructive ways.*

Everybody kind of perceives me as being angry. It's not anger, it's motivation.

—Roger Clemens

Anger is not a threat to our recovery, but our failure to channel it and use it well is. Some things deserve anger and should be our targets. Injustice and disrespect to our fellow human beings is a prime example. Out-of-control anger, however, does not serve anyone well.

We can achieve greater peace of mind when we learn to manage our anger rather than hide it. When we learn to focus our anger at worthy targets and express it clearly and directly, without stooping to abusive language or threats, we become much more effective men. That way, anger can be a constructive source of energy and we can hope to resolve it and make things better. We are learning to take our own inventories and to be honest with ourselves about all of our feelings.

Today I will examine myself for my angry feelings and make wise choices about how to manage them.

*Be what you is, cuz if you be what you ain't, then you
ain't what you is.*

—Tombstone inscription, Tombstone, Arizona

When a young man was worried about how to get a
special woman to like him, he talked to his grandfather about it. The advice his grandfather gave him
was, "Just be yourself." That was easier said than done,
but it was good advice. In order to be ourselves, we
must first get to know ourselves and then make peace
with who we are.

In taking an inventory of ourselves, in admitting
our faults and our strengths, and in facing those we
have harmed and repairing our mistakes, we are discovering ourselves and accepting ourselves. That is how
we fill out our true manhood. No one stands taller
than the man who knows himself, with all his weaknesses and all his assets, and accepts himself as he is.

*Today I accept myself and continue to grow into a
better person.*

*God brought light out of darkness, not out of lesser light;
God can bring thy summer out of winter, though thou
     have no spring.
All occasions invite God's mercies, and all times are
     God's seasons.*

—John Donne

Despair has been no stranger to many of us. We recall
times when all spirit and all hope seemed to evaporate.
We may still be subject to dark moods. In our bleakest
moments, we wonder where to turn for hope. We may
see no reason for optimism as we look at our situation.
In those difficult times we are most in need of the support of God, our Higher Power. The greatest spiritual
teachers and all the world's great religions tell us that
God is present to those most in need.

In our darkest hours, God is with us, within us, beside us, supporting us. Perhaps we experience the presence of God in a call to a friend, a bird lighting on a
branch, or a beautiful song on the radio. And out of
darkness comes light. Today's difficulties are only one
moment in the flow of our lives and they will change.

Today is another occasion that invites God's mercies.

Courage is not the absence of despair; it is, rather the capacity to move ahead in spite of despair.

—Rollo May

Some days we wake up to overwhelming feelings that things look bleak. We see loss and danger around us, and we fear for the future. That is when our character is most tested. That is when we are called to continue to just put one foot in front of the other. There is no need to solve all our problems right away or to change the world immediately. Courage isn't necessarily a feeling of confidence that we can triumph over all odds. It's knowing that we can move ahead one step at a time, and it's taking positive action in the face of our fears.

Each day we can do small things that are constructive. By these small things, we can place ourselves on the positive side of life's equation. We can put our weight where we want to go. That is courage.

Today, in the face of my despair, I will focus my efforts on the side of my hopes and values.

Hear me, four quarters of the world—a relative I am!
Give me the strength to walk the soft earth, a relative to
all that is! Give me the eyes to see and the strength to
understand, that I may be like you. With your power
only can I face the winds.

—Black Elk

All of nature upholds us. It is inevitable that we face strong winds in our lives. These winds challenge us with losses, sadness, difficulties at our work, frightening dangers, and desires for things that only hurt us.

Our spiritual program teaches us that we are not alone. Nature surrounds us. Perhaps we have never considered that the bird sitting on the branch is our relative. It breathes air and has warm blood flowing through its veins just as we do. Even the tall tree we walk past each day is part of our family of life. These beings comfort us and can teach us about how to live. Does the fox in the field worry about what he will eat next week? No, he only hunts for what he needs today.

I will open myself to the whole family of life, to
the lessons I can learn, and to the strength that it
can give me.

We make a living by what we get, but we make a life by what we give.

—Winston Churchill

As we grow spiritually, we naturally become more generous. It's a quality of a well-developed person. Rather than being anxious over whether we will have enough—and rather than hungrily seeking more and more—we become more openhearted. We feel more abundant within ourselves and find that our spirit of generosity even adds to our own abundant feelings. Where we see a need, we help out.

A generous person doesn't need to shower others with material gifts. The most precious gifts are things such as paying attention to others, respecting them for who they are, and giving our time. Often a material gift is a symbol of the good feelings in a relationship. In our generosity, we also learn to receive others' gifts to us with humility and respect.

Today I take pleasure in my spirit of generosity.

The miracle is this—the more we share, the more we have.

—Leonard Nimoy

Look around you at the happiest people you know. They are also the most generous and giving people. A generous spirit creates its own environment. In recovery we talk a lot about gratitude—and we have a lot to be grateful for. This feeling of gratitude inspires us to be generous toward others in many different ways. Most sharing is not of material things but a sharing of our spirit, our forgiveness, and our respect for others.

We can cultivate a generous spirit by reminding ourselves that we have enough. We have enough to live well, we are surrounded by love, we have been forgiven for many wrongs that we committed, and life is filled with interesting adventure. When we share from this sense of abundance, our feeling of well-being only grows.

Today I will be generous and sharing toward the other people I come into contact with.

*The day the child realizes that all adults are imperfect
he becomes an adolescent; the day he forgives them
he becomes an adult; the day he forgives himself he
becomes wise.*

—Alden Nowlan

Facing up to our wrongs is a foundation stone in our recovery. We have been contending with imperfection since the day we were born, both in ourselves and in others. Forgiveness is central to this whole process. When we admit that we have made a mistake, we affirm our belief in our values at the same time. Nothing is more honorable than saying that we hold a value and admitting that we fell short of it. That guilt is the pathway back to repair and forgiveness.

Shame is a dead-end emotion in which forgiveness doesn't seem possible. In our recovery we are turning shame into guilt, making repair where it is possible and accepting forgiveness or forgiving ourselves. For many men, accepting forgiveness from ourselves or others is the hardest thing to do. It takes true humility to receive forgiveness because we are admitting that we are imperfect like everyone else; to defy the forgiveness that is available to us is arrogant.

*Today I will try to forgive myself for the ways I have
violated my own values.*

*One of the goals of spiritual practice is to make
conscious what was previously unconscious.*

—Dan Millman

We find as we proceed with our recovery that commitment to honesty reveals more to ourselves than to anyone else. We begin by taking the advice of our program to be honest with others as well as ourselves. To our surprise, we realize how much we had hidden from even ourselves. It's called denial. We sincerely missed seeing the elephant that was walking around in the living room. We honestly didn't see what we didn't want to see.

Spiritual practice teaches us to yield to the guidance of our Higher Power and to stop controlling. When we yield in that way and when we are willing to see the truth, we feel that we have awakened. We are amazed at what we now see.

*Today I am grateful for my spiritual awakening and
for the truth it allows me to see.*

The spiritual life is about becoming more at home in your own skin.

—Parker J. Palmer

We will not feel serene and at peace with the world every day. Some days we feel distressed and restless and we want something we may not even be able to name. At their most intense, these feelings are like ravenous hunger or dark dread. We may wish we could escape into another reality—or into the "unreality" of co-dependency or addiction. But now we have the opportunity to use better, more satisfying methods of coping.

When we look at these feelings as spiritual needs, we can use spiritual principles to achieve peace of mind. We can make contact with a trusted friend who will listen respectfully to our feelings. We can remember that our Higher Power is always with us, and we can take quiet time for meditation and reflection. We can spend some time where we feel most connected with God—walking outdoors among trees and gardens, listening to music, or going for a good workout. After we respond to distressed feelings in this way, we get relief and grow stronger without the negatives of our old escapes.

Today I will follow the spiritual principles that nurture my life and make me feel better.

Apathy is the behavior of a slave.

—Richard Wagenvoord

When we were slaves to addiction and codependency, our values were suppressed and our enthusiasm for life was dampened. We were under the influence of our addictive brain. The prospect of life without our substance and without our controlling behavior seemed dull and very scary.

In recovery, we also recover from dullness and apathy. Life gets interesting and full of possibilities. We shed our turned-off attitude. We drop our cynicism and become believers, open to interesting and exciting opportunities. Having faced our slavery and found a path to freedom, the world opens up to us. We know we have a lot of work to do, but we are willing to suspend our doubts. We see that life can be better for us. Apathy has been replaced by hope and a deep sense of gratitude.

Today I can see a path to follow that makes me hopeful and I am full of gratitude for my freedom.

*Being on the tightrope is living; everything else
is waiting.*

—Karl Wallenda

In walking a tightrope, a person has to learn to relax
while going forward in a situation filled with risk. If he
is tense and keeps his body rigid, he will lose his balance and fall. But if he stays relaxed and keeps his
muscles loose while remaining very focused, he can
continuously respond and readjust his balance while
walking. Then he will experience the exhilaration of
success. This is a perfect metaphor for life itself, for
growing in an intimate relationship and for growing in
recovery.

Life itself is a risk. When we hold on too tight, remain too guarded, and anxiously try to control every
factor, we become stiff and reactive rather than calm,
focused, and responsive. The guidance of this path
teaches us to let go of our anxieties and leads us to
peace of mind. When we learn to do that, we can deftly
walk our path and more effectively maintain our balance in dealing with whatever comes up.

Today I will calm myself while walking on my path.

*You cannot step twice into the same river, for other
waters are continually flowing on.*

—Heraclitus

On this last day of the year, time is on our minds. Naturally, we look back at the year just passing. Whether we feel grateful that it is over, or grateful for the gifts it brought, we can always be grateful to be in this healing program on this day. Some of us took our first Steps in recovery this year and others marked another year among many years. Once on the path, the critical fact is that we are all brothers, equally seeking the same goal: a sober life and peace of mind.

New Year's Eve is a time for celebrations and parties. For some of us, New Year's Eve in the past was a day of complete immersion in our addiction and codependency. There is no point in giving much attention to regrets. Today our celebration has a deeper spiritual meaning. It's a good time to take stock of how far we have come and for gratitude for the benefits of our recovery. We can look at the challenges we faced and what we learned from them. We can look at the gifts that came into our lives.

*Today I thank God for the gifts that continue to flow
and enhance my life.*

☐ The Twelve Steps of Alcoholics ☐ ☐ ☐ ☐ ☐ ☐
Anonymous*

1. We admitted we were powerless over alcohol—that our lives had become unmanageable.
2. Came to believe that a Power greater than ourselves could restore us to sanity.
3. Made a decision to turn our will and our lives over to the care of God *as we understood Him.*
4. Made a searching and fearless moral inventory of ourselves.
5. Admitted to God, to ourselves, and to another human being the exact nature of our wrongs.
6. Were entirely ready to have God remove all these defects of character.
7. Humbly asked Him to remove our shortcomings.
8. Made a list of all persons we had harmed, and became willing to make amends to them all.
9. Made direct amends to such people wherever possible, except when to do so would injure them or others.
10. Continued to take personal inventory and when we were wrong promptly admitted it.
11. Sought through prayer and meditation to improve our conscious contact with God *as we understood Him,* praying only for knowledge of His will for us and the power to carry that out.
12. Having had a spiritual awakening as the result of these steps, we tried to carry this message to alcoholics, and to practice these principles in all our affairs.

*From *Alcoholics Anonymous,* 4th ed., published by AA World Services, Inc., New York, N.Y., 59-60.

Hazelden Publishing and Educational Services is a division of the Hazelden Foundation, a not-for-profit organization. Since 1949, Hazelden has been a leader in promoting the dignity and treatment of people afflicted with the disease of chemical dependency.

The mission of the foundation is to improve the quality of life for individuals, families, and communities by providing a national continuum of information, education, and recovery services that are widely accessible; to advance the field through research and training; and to improve our quality and effectiveness through continuous improvement and innovation.

Stemming from that, the mission of this division is to provide quality information and support to people wherever they may be in their personal journey—from education and early intervention, through treatment and recovery, to personal and spiritual growth.

Although our treatment programs do not necessarily use everything Hazelden publishes, our bibliotherapeutic materials support our mission and the Twelve Step philosophy upon which it is based. We encourage your comments and feedback.

The headquarters of the Hazelden Foundation are in Center City, Minnesota. Additional treatment facilities are located in Chicago, Illinois; Newberg, Oregon; New York, New York; Plymouth, Minnesota; and St. Paul, Minnesota. At these sites, we provide a continuum of care for men and women of all ages. Our Plymouth facility is designed specifically for youth and families.

For more information on Hazelden, please call **1-800-257-7800**. Or you may access our World Wide Web site on the Internet at **www.hazelden.org**.